Debates in Economic History

Edited by Peter Mathias

The Causes of the Industrial Revolution in England

The Causes of the
Industrial Revolution
in England

edited with an introduction by
R. M. HARTWELL

METHUEN & CO LTD
11 NEW FETTER LANE LONDON EC 4

First published 1967 by Methuen & Co Ltd
Reprinted 1968
Reprinted 1970
Reprinted 1972
Introduction © 1967 by R. M. Hartwell
Printed in Great Britain by
Fletcher & Son Ltd, Norwich
(Hardback) SBN 416 47990 1
(Paperback) SBN 416 48000 4

Distributed in the USA by
HARPER & ROW PUBLISHERS INC
BARNES & NOBLE IMPORT DIVISION

Contents

Preface

The Industrial Revolution, as Dr Hartwell stresses, marks one of the great watersheds in the history of human society. The elemental conditions of any country's population before the modernization of its economy has been poverty: life on the margins of subsistence as an inescapable fate for the masses of any nation. A minority, enjoying the economic surplus produced from land or office, trade or taxes, may well be able to live in extreme luxury. There may well be magnificent cultural monuments and very wealthy religious institutions. But, with low productivity – low output per head – in a traditionally conducted agriculture, in any economy which has agriculture as the mainspring of its national income and the main source of employment the economic system as a whole does not produce much above subsistence needs. And most of what is produced beyond the immediate consumption needs of those who produce it, flows into various forms of conspicuous expenditure and consumption rather than into productive investment. The population as a whole, whether of medieval Europe or nineteenth-century India, lives close to the tyranny of nature, under the threat of harvest failure or disease. Increasing numbers in these circumstances, if there is a shortage of fertile land workable under the traditional methods, will eventually bring checks. Even if one looks to late fourteenth- and fifteenth-century England as the 'golden age' of the labourer – as did Thorold Rogers – it is to see good purchasing power for wages in the aftermath of a decimation of population, which is as though one would advocate the solution of India's present difficulties by famine and disease and count it a success to raise *per capita* income by lessening the number of people alive rather than by expanding the economy. Even if population establishes an equilibrium with resources, through various types of social control, it will be an equilibrium at a very low level of real income. National poverty of this sort cannot be solved by the redistribution of income, only by enlarging the total output of the economy. And to increase the national income as a whole, and productivity per head, means changing the nature of the economic system. For this reason the Industrial Revolution, which focused the initial stages of this rapid transformation in Britain (though not, of course, denying the long economic evolution of Western Europe through to the eighteenth century) is a fundamental divide in the economic development of the country, marking a break with a tradition of economic life and a pace of change which had lasted for centuries and which, in certain essential characteristics, had been universal across all countries of the globe up to that time. It is not accidental that the actual term was given currency in the early nineteenth century in France by an economist who explicitly claimed that since the late eighteenth century deep-seated changes of this nature were affecting Britain as fundamental in their effects upon the national life, although operating in a less dramatic way, as the political upheavals which had changed the face of France in 1789.

Any term used to represent a complex historical process runs a semantic hazard when it becomes common currency – the Renaissance and the Baroque no less than the Industrial Revolution. To a degree the criteria used to designate the term remain subjective, and hence raise no more problems methodologically than those of ascertaining whether the data fit appropriately into the chosen boxes. But the choice of criteria itself comes into question. As long as the term 'Industrial Revolution' is interpreted loosely, to mean technical changes which transformed productive processes (or a single process) in an industry, then its origins become lost in the mists of time. Technical changes of this order, although varying dramatically in pace and extent, form a continuum in economic history, so that, thus defined, the concept is universalized, potentially robbed of limitations as to time and space. (The earliest of a succession of 'Industrial Revolutions', thus conceived, is that of 'the late Bronze Age'.) Only when one adopts the more rigorous definition of the beginnings of higher growth rates of industrial production generally (involving technical change, rising investment, and productivity) and of the onset, through this, of cumulative structural changes in the economy, with the complex of relationships that lie behind this, does the term take on a more specific significance.

In another way the metaphor of 'revolution' creates certain difficulties. It implies a greater speed of change in the short run than certain recent attempts to measure it are sometimes held to justify – although this is, again, a subjective criterion, and judged against a perspective of the whole sweep of history, the adjective revolutionary is surely appropriate. Equally it is misleading to force the parallel with a political event – a single, once-and-for-all phenomenon – because the Industrial Revolution is rather the initiating phases of a continuing sequence. Thus are born other semantic and definitional problems of the 'second' and succeeding 'industrial revolutions' which 'stage' theories of historical change usually occasion.

Judged against the criteria of the onset of higher rates of industrial growth and structural change, as Dr Hartwell claims, eighteenth-century England, building upon the previous slow processes of development which had been distinguishing Europe from all other societies, saw the emergence of new economic forces of momentous import. For these reasons the Industrial Revolution has become a focus of interest for all economic historians, economists, and other social scientists concerned with the problems of initiating and fostering economic growth in the 'third world' today. For if the Industrial Revolution stands at one of the great watersheds of history it marks also the greatest divide in the contemporary world – that between the poor and the rich nations.

PETER MATHIAS

Acknowledgements

The editor and publishers wish to thank the following for permission to reproduce the articles listed below:

Professor F. Crouzet for 'England and France in the Eighteenth Century: A Comparative Analysis of two Economic Growths' (translated by Mrs J. Sondheimer from *Annales*, Vol. XXI, No 2, 1966); Miss Phyllis Deane for 'The Industrial Revolution and Economic Growth: The Evidence of Early British National Income Estimates' (*Economic Development and Cultural Change*, Vol. V, No. 1, 1957, published by the University of Chicago Press); Dr Elizabeth W. Gilboy for 'Demand as a Factor in the Industrial Revolution' (from *Facts and Factors in Economic History*, Harvard University Press, 1932); Dr R. M. Hartwell for 'The Causes of the Industrial Revolution: An Essay in Methodology' (*The Economic History Review*, 2nd series, Vol. XVIII, No. 1, 1965); the Macmillan Company for 'Industrial Revolution', by Professor Herbert Heaton (from *Encyclopaedia of the Social Sciences*, Vol. VIII, 1933, copyright 1932 by the Macmillan Company, renewed 1960 by the Macmillan Company); E. A. Wrigley for 'Supply of Raw Materials in the Industrial Revolution' (*The Economic History Review*, 2nd series, Vol. XVIII, No. 1, 1965).

1 Introduction

On any historical accounting the industrial revolution of England began one of the great discontinuities of history, marking 'the great divide' between a world of slow economic growth, in which population and real incomes were increasing slowly or not at all, and a world of much faster economic growth, in which population has increased at an almost frightening rate and in which there have been sustained increases in real income per head. In a stimulating book on *The Economic History of World Population*,[1] Carlo Cipolla has argued that mankind's economic history can be written largely in terms of two revolutions which fundamentally altered the economic and demographic levels of human endeavour, and which on both occasions made possible long-term economic growth. These two revolutions were, first, the agricultural revolution of the eighth millennium B.C. which by 1500–2000 B.C. had converted man from hunter and food-gatherer to farmer; and second, the industrial revolution beginning in the eighteenth century which in two centuries radically reduced the proportion of the world's population engaged in agriculture (80–90 per cent in 1750 to 50–60 per cent in 1950) and converted man increasingly from farmer into maker of services and manufactured goods. This conversion, which has been described generally as industrialization, has vastly increased the resources available to mankind and has allowed (perhaps caused) a population explosion. The agricultural revolution had also lifted the limits to population growth, so that in the 10 to 12,000 years which separated it from the industrial revolution, world population grew from what must have been a maximum of 20 millions in 10,000 B.C. to 750 ± 100 millions in 1750. With industrialization, however, population growth was much faster. By 1850 world population

[1] Pelican Book, A537 (London, 1962).

had grown to 1,200 ± 100 millions, by 1900 to 1,600 ± 100 millions, and by 1950 to 2,500 millions; at the present impressive rate of growth world population will double in the next forty years.

If the limit to world population of the pre-industrial revolution world was around 1,000 millions, the limit of the industrial world, in spite of much argument and calculation, has not yet been reckoned. So far world population under industrialization has increased at the same time as much of it has bettered its standard of living, but it is difficult not to foresee a situation in which further population growth will be possible only at the expense of a deterioration in living standards. This possibility poses one of the most interesting and unanswered questions in economic history: the extent to which a balance between income and population has restrained growth in the past, and the extent to which industrialization has represented an escape – perhaps the only escape – from 'the Malthusian Trap', the situation in which population growth has been limited by, and has also limited, economic growth. The industrial revolution in England, and in other countries which have industrialized, resulted in more people with more goods. In other words, the industrial revolution was an example of successful growth, the achievement of 'the growth of output per head of population'.[1] This was its significant economic result, whatever the mechanism which enabled such growth, and however difficult the process of such growth is to analyse.

Economists and historians are both interested in economic growth. The economists are seeking prescriptions for growth, and look forward to the day when they will be able to draw up a blueprint for the growth of any particular economy. The historians, for a long time, did not consciously regard what they were studying to have been, in varying degrees, case-studies or aspects of economic growth (and, sometimes, economic stagnation or decline). The main reason for the economists' interest in growth stems directly from their interest in the problems of the underdeveloped economies of the world. This

[1] For example, this is the subject matter of his book, as defined by W. A. Lewis in *The Theory of Economic Growth* (London, 1955), p. 9.

interest has been stimulated, also, by realizing that the liberal economic philosophy of the nineteenth century, which reckoned that free enterprise and free trade would inevitably result in economic growth, of the Western pattern, all over the world, has not had that result; and also by the emergence of a different economic philosophy and a different social system which claim to be more efficient in promoting growth, a philosophy and a system which exists, for example, in Soviet Russia.[1] The historians' interest in growth is prompted partly by the economist, but partly also by the realization that much of what they have been doing in the past has been the documenting and describing of economic growth.

II

With a quickening interest in growth, it was inevitable that both economists and historians should look more closely at the industrial revolution in England. Of all the historical examples of growth, none is more important or more interesting than the industrial revolution in England: it was the first industrial revolution; it led to the first example of modern economic growth; it was a growth achieved mainly without external assistance; it was growth in the context of a free enterprise economy; it was growth accompanied by a social and political revolution which were achieved with little violence; it was 'the engine of growth' for other economies, stimulating them by example, by the export of men and capital, and by trade. In spite of its obvious importance, however, surprisingly little effort has been made, by either historians or economists, to explain why the industrial revolution occurred. Indeed, on the causes of the industrial revolution there has been little formal debate, even though every historian who has written about the industrial revolution has talked about causes. In so far as there has been a modern debate, it has tended to be commentaries on, or reactions to, W. W. Rostow's article 'The take-off into self-sustained

---

[1] See S. Kuznets, *Economic Growth and Structure* (London, 1965), Chapter I, for an account of the reasons for the current interest in economic growth.

growth' of 1956,[1] and his book, *The Stages of Economic Growth* of 1960.[2] Indeed, Rostow can reasonably claim to be the most influential of modern economic historians, whose phrase 'the take-off' has passed into everyday speech, and whose theories about growth (and the industrial revolution) have inspired a spate of literature, largely critical, of which contributions by the following historians and economists are the most relevant to the theme of this book: A. K. Cairncross, H. J. Habakkuk and Phyllis Deane, P. A. Baran and E. J. Hobsbawm, and A. Fishlow.[3]

Other general discussions about the causes of the industrial revolution in England are to be found also in the now vast literature on economic development.[4] This literature, however, is for and by economists and administrators interested in the problems of the contemporary underdeveloped world; as such it is not so much concerned with a systematic historical analysis of English economic growth as with extracting from English experience some of the secrets of successful growth. There is no doubt, however, that the economists' preoccupation with growth has jolted the historians into a more careful and more explicitly theoretical analysis of the causes of English growth. Nevertheless, there is still only one book which has taken 'the long view of British economic growth', *British Economic Growth, 1688–1959. Trends and Structure* by Phyllis Deane and W. A. Cole, in which, also, an ingenious attempt is made to describe

[1] *Economic Journal*, LXVI, 1956.

[2] Cambridge University Press, 1960.

[3] A. K. Cairncross, 'The Stages of Economic Growth', *The Economic History Review*, 2nd series, XIII, 1961; H. J. Habakkuk and P. Deane, 'The Take-off in Britain', *The Economics of Take-off into Sustained Growth*, W. W. Rostow (ed.) (London, 1963); P. A. Baran and E. J. Hobsbawm, 'The Stages of Economic Growth', *Kyklos*, XIV, 1961; A. Fishlow, 'Empty Economic Stages', *Economic Journal*, LXXV, 1965.

[4] For example: S. Kuznets, 'Underdeveloped Countries and the Pre-Industrial Phase in the Advanced Countries: an Attempt at Comparison', *The Economics of Underdevelopment*, A. N. Agarwala and S. P. Singh (eds.) (New York, 1963); H. J. Habakkuk, 'Historical Experience of Economic Development', *Problems in Economic Development*, E. A. G. Robinson (ed.) (London, 1965); G. M. Meier and R. E. Baldwin, *Economic Development. Theory, History, Policy* (New York, 1957), Part 2; N. S. Buchanan and H. S. Ellis, *Approaches to Economic Development* (New York, 1955), Chapter 7.

'the mechanics of eighteenth-century growth'.[1] Before this, perhaps the only important general essay on the causes of the industrial revolution was by T. S. Ashton, in the first chapter of his remarkable classic, *The Industrial Revolution*, of 1948.[2] Indeed, a general consideration of the various attempts to explain the industrial revolution, in the form of a reasonably comprehensive and critical survey of the writings of economic historians on the subject, was not published until 1965[3] (in the article 'The Causes of the Industrial Revolution. An Essay in Methodology', reproduced in this volume). Since then, however, at least four further general contributions have appeared: Phyllis Deane's *The First Industrial Revolution*,[4] D. S. Landes' 'Technological Change and Development in Western Europe, 1750–1914',[5] M. W. Flinn's *Origins of the Industrial Revolution*,[6] and Charles Wilson's *England's Apprenticeship, 1603–1763*,[7] the last volume being by far the most important recent attempt to explain the origins of English industrialization.

Debate on the causes of the industrial revolution before this very recent literature took the form, usually, of argument about mono-causal explanations, with each contribution expounding or criticizing a particular theory of growth. The result was a series of confrontations, each ending in indecision or confusion.[8] In so far as multi-causal explanations were attempted, these were not challenged so much as rivalled; each explanation consisted of a list of relevant 'factors' or 'forces' for growth, but not of an explicit model of growth with functionally related variables. These lists varied in content and comprehensiveness,

[1] Cambridge University Press, 1962, Chapter 2, Section 5.
[2] Oxford University Press, 1948.
[3] *The Economic History Review*, 2nd series, XVIII (1965).
[4] Cambridge University Press, 1965.
[5] *The Cambridge Economic History of Europe*, Vol. VI, 1965.
[6] London, 1966.   [7] London, 1965.
[8] A good example of such a debate was in July 1961 when a *Past and Present* conference discussed 'the origins of the industrial revolution' (the proceedings being summarized in *Past and Present*, no. 17, 1961). If the published summary is accurate, obviously the discussion was unsystematic and inconclusive, and did nothing to further understanding of the causes of the industrial revolution, even though the conference was attended by a large and representative group of British economic historians.

B

but because their constituent elements were not related in an explanatory mechanism, there were no obvious criteria by which one list could be judged superior to any other for explaining why the industrial revolution occurred when, where, and how it did. The lists were non-operational and qualitative, and so there was little reason to choose between them.[1] Nevertheless every attempt to determine the causes of the industrial revolution, to relate cause and effect, did assume, at least implicitly, a model of growth; for example, as in the most popular theory, a simple capital accumulation model, in which increasing capital formation led to the industrial revolution.

The main weaknesses of the historians' approach, however, were, first, a failure to define 'the industrial revolution', and second, a failure to use economic theory to make explicit the growth models being used (and, consequently, the relevant variables in those models, and the relationships between variables). Obviously a term which was used to describe overall change in an economy and society over a century presented the historian with an almost impossible task of explanation. The very magnitude of the problem of determining cause and effect on this scale led inevitably to irresponsibility; almost any factor which was changing could be, and was assumed to have been a relevant variable of growth, and prejudice operated with rationality to favour this variable or that, and thus to increase speculation rather than understanding. Obviously, therefore, it is now necessary to specify the problem we are investigating; i.e. to define the economic phenomenon whose causes we are seeking. Then, and only then, can we set about the problem of explanation, of constructing an appropriate economic model of the industrial revolution in England.

III

It is surprising that so little thought has gone into a definition of 'the industrial revolution'. In so far as the words constitute

---

[1] A good example is E. Lipson, *The Growth of English Society* (London, 1949), pp. 190–3, where he lists five reasons for England's leadership in industrialization.

no more than 'a handy phrase for describing a period',[1] then no precise definition is possible (or necessary). The requirements of the economic historian, however, demand a definition of the industrial revolution which both isolates its essential economic characteristics and which also locates it in time. Undoubtedly, the industrial revolution was an example of what is now called 'economic growth', and its essential characteristic was an unprecedented and sustained increase in the rate of growth of the output of goods and services. This seems so obvious that we must ask why the historians have not always looked at the industrial revolution in this way. The reason is that they were long inhibited by preoccupation with the problems of distribution and consumption rather than with explaining the increase in output. The increase in output was assumed rather than examined; it was a *datum* and attention focused on how the output was distributed. On distribution, also, there was another assumption: that, even though output grew, the consumption of the mass of the people declined. Of course it is possible for output to grow while consumption declines, but it is not a necessary consequence of the growth of output. However, there was no explicit consideration of the models of growth compatible with declining consumption.[2]

Thus two large assumptions, relatively unquestioned, inhibited research both into the process of growth and also into what happened to consumption and distribution during growth. There was instead a concentration of interest on 'the social costs' of industrialization, leading to detailed research into the working and living conditions of the labouring poor in an industrializing economy.[3] Such research revealed a generally squalid picture of working-class life, but it was a static picture. What working-class life *before* the industrial revolution was like was not seriously examined; what it was like *after* the industrial revolution was used only as a contrast with conditions during the revolution; conditions before, during, and after the

[1] G. N. Clark, *The Idea of the Industrial Revolution* (Glasgow, 1953), pp. 32-3.
[2] See R. M. Hartwell, 'The Rising Standard of Living in England, 1800-1850', *The Economic History Review*, 2nd series, XIII, No. 3 (1961).
[3] The most famous books are the labourer volumes of J. L. and B. Hammond, on the village, town, and skilled labourers.

industrial revolution were not seen as part of a secular trend in the improvement of life, the beginning of which preceded industrialization.

The obvious and essential character of the industrial revolution was *the sustained increase in the rate of growth of total and* per capita *output at a rate which was revolutionary compared with what went before*. Between 1780 and 1850 the growth of national product per head – the best simple measure of economic growth – averaged from 1 to 1½ per cent per annum; i.e. output grew at a rate which doubled real output per head every fifty years, and increased it more than fourfold over the nineteenth century. This is the phenomenon to be explained: this remarkable increase in output. Now the output of goods and services in any economy depends on the human and natural resources of that economy, and on the application of human effort to those resources. There can be a growth of output, in total and *per capita*, for two reasons: first, from an increase in resources, and second, because of an improvement in the productivity of human effort. Obviously at any time the resources of an economy are given, and can only be increased over time by human effort. But there are in all economies under-used or unused resources (for example, land and minerals), and there can be an increase in total output merely by bringing these resources into use without necessarily any improvement in the methods of their exploitation. Output can thus expand without any increase in human efficiency. For example, an increase in population will almost certainly increase output by increasing labour supply, but it will not necessarily increase *per capita* output. The crucial characteristic of growth is an increase in output *per capita*, and this occurs only when men are more efficient in exploiting the resources at their command.[1] Human effort can be made more productive in three main ways: first, by *invention and innovation* (by the discovery and application of new knowledge to production); second, by *economy* (by the better use and organization of existing equipment and resources); and third, by *increasing the amount of capital* (by increasing the level of pro-

---

[1] Except, as E. L. Jones has reminded me, when fortuitous changes in climate and animal populations give mankind short-term windfalls.

ductive investment, either in humans or in equipment, and thus
by making men more efficient either in themselves or because
of the equipment they have to work with).

The problems of explaining the industrial revolution can
now be made explicit. First, it is necessary to determine when
the sustained increase in the rate of growth of output began, so
that we can have a terminal limiting date to our inquiries.
Second, we must trace the growth of inputs of resources, to see
what factor inputs increased, when and, if possible, why. This
will be a task, particularly, of determining the growth of population, of land use and of raw material exploitation. Third, we
must inquire into the history of invention (and innovation).
This is particularly important because changing technology has
often been given as the main reason for the increase in output;
the industrial revolution is thus seen mainly as a decisive technological breakthrough. Fourth, changes in the organization of
commerce, finance, and industry, which made them more
efficient, must be examined to show, for example, how the
market economy functioned more rationally. Fifth, the growth
of savings and the accumulation of physical capital has to be
described and measured. Sixth, it is necessary to show how
England's 'human capital' improved, how it became more
skilled, more market-oriented, and more economically adven-
turous. Finally, the changing structure of the economy, and the
consequent changes in the composition of output, have to be
mapped to give us the chronology of change and some idea of
why change occurred. With this information it should be possible to devise a model of growth which would explain the
industrial revolution. Since, however, we do not yet have all
this information, and certainly not in quantified form, any
model of the industrial revolution will necessarily be specula-
tive, with relationships stated in qualitative rather than in
quantitative–functional terms. This is not to say that more precise relationships can never be established; only that more research, especially to give quantitative precision to variables, is
necessary before precise relationships can be defined, and a
statistically verifiable model of eighteenth-century growth can
be formulated.

IV

In order to understand the literature of the industrial revolution, and to judge the value of particular contributions, it is important to distinguish those parts of analyses which concentrate on identifying relevant variables of growth, and those which are more specifically concerned with the process of growth, with how the variables interact to produce growth. The abiding impression of the writing about variables, in spite of the featuring of an impressively wide variety of factors, is the determination of each historian to concentrate on one variable. This, in part, explains the relative neglect of process analysis: concentration on one variable usually implies a mono-causal model of growth; such a model is easy to understand and is conceptually satisfying, in addition to being a powerful analytical tool. A full range of variables is listed below,[1] but most historians have come down in favour of one or more of the following causes of the industrial revolution: an increase in the rate of capital formation (either because of low interest rates encouraging investment, or because of profit inflation); an increase in world trade (the natural result of an expanding geographical frontier), in which England gained disproportionately (thus stimulating export industries, and, finally, general growth); a technological revolution (the result of an autonomous increase in knowledge, the application of which transformed the machinery and organization of industry, making it much more productive); and growth of *laissez-faire* and of a rational ethic towards wealth (the result of changes both in philosophic and religious convictions), which liberalized the context and possibilities of enterprise. There has been a tendency also, to regard the last three of these factors as being stimuli external to the economy, exogenously determined variables impacting on the economy to produce growth. This has made the problem of *economic* explanation seem easy: the first cause is a *deus ex machina* and the problem becomes one of explaining the adaptation of the economy to the prime mover.

However, before considering whether the individual causes

[1] In Chapter 3.

listed above could have produced growth, let us consider what the historians have said more generally about the process of growth. On the process of growth the historians have been almost invariably vague and analytically unhelpful. Nevertheless three controversies about *how* the industrial revolution occurred, indicate clearly that implicit in the historians' analyses are theories about the process of change in the eighteenth century. These controversies have been concerned with: first, the dating of the turning-point of the industrial revolution; second, the basis from which industrialization began; and third, the stages of growth which led up to industrialization.

The first controversy is really between *evolutionist* and *revolutionist*, between those who see the industrial revolution as the unspectacular climax of an evolutionary process, the consequence of a long period of slow economic growth, and those who see a clear discontinuity in English economic history, an obvious turning-point, a revolution after which industrialization proceeded apace, gathering momentum for sustained growth within a generation of effort. The traditional view was revolutionary. H. de B. Gibbons, writing in 1896, wrote: 'The change . . . was sudden and violent. The great inventions were all made in a comparatively short space of time. . . . In little more than twenty years all the great inventions of Watt, Arkwright, and Boulton had been completed, . . . and the modern factory system had fairly begun.'[1] The view that the industrial revolution *began* in 1760 was early enshrined in the textbooks, and in specialist writing, for example in the influential books of the Hammonds. But already by 1912 W. J. Ashley objected that the industrial revolution 'did but carry further, though on a far greater scale and with far greater rapidity, changes which had been proceeding long before'.[2] More recently alternative starting-dates have been given, 1780 by J. U. Nef and T. S. Ashton,[3] and 1740 by P. Deane and W. A. Cole.[4] Dispute about

[1] H. de B. Gibbons, *Industry in England* (London, 1897), p. 341.

[2] W. J. Ashley, *The Economic Organization of England* (London, 1914), p. 141.

[3] J. U. Nef, 'The Industrial Revolution Reconsidered', *Journal of Economic History*, III (1943), p. 5; T. S. Ashton, *An Economic History of England. The 18th Century* (London, 1955), p. 125.

[4] P. Deane and W. A. Cole, *British Economic Growth, 1688–1959*, op. cit., p. 82.

the date of the turning-point, with claimants differing by as much as forty years, indicates not only that the turning-point is difficult to locate but also that its very existence must be doubted. Nevertheless, the most persuasive of revolutionists is a recent writer, W. W. Rostow. Indeed, Rostow invented the phrase 'the take-off' to emphasize his thesis that an industrial revolution is 'a decisive breakthrough' which takes place quickly, during which 'compound interest gets built into society's structure'.[1] The reaction of historians and economists to Rostow has been, on this point at least, sceptical; 'they have grown accustomed to emphasizing the continuity of historical change, to tracing back to a previous age the forces producing a social explosion, and to explaining away the apparent leaps in economic development'.[2]

But are evolutionist and revolutionist so irreconcilable? Does not their difference arise, in part at least, from a failure to make clear what was being revolutionized? Was it the economy, or was it industry? There is no doubt that there was an important turning-point in the rate of growth of industrial output in the 1780s.[3] Taking a longer view, say from 1750 to 1850, there was also obviously a revolution in the structure of the economy, in the composition of total output, and in the distribution of employment, which gives concrete meaning to the idea of an economic revolution. However, the turning-point in the rate of growth of industrial production in the 1780s can hardly be discerned in the growth figures of the national income, so small at that date was the contribution of the new industrial output to national income. The 1780s marked the climax of a slow steady process of economic growth in which the pressure of industrial demand finally hit

---

[1] *The Stages of Economic Growth*, op. cit., p. 36. The mechanism for change is an increased savings rate from 5 to 10 or more per cent of the national income.

[2] A. K. Cairncross, *Factors in Economic Development* (London, 1962), p. 138.

[3] The evidence for this was first explicitly stated by J. U. Nef, in terms of important inventions of the 1780s (the rotary motion steam engine, the puddling-process for the production of iron, the perfection of cotton-spinning machinery) which enabled production increases, and developed further by T. S. Ashton, in terms of output figures ('after 1782 almost every statistical series of production shows a sharp upward turn'). 'The Industrial Revolution Reconsidered', op. cit., p. 24, and 'An Economic History of England', op. cit., p. 125.

the ceiling of production possibilities in a number of strategic industries with the techniques of the pre-industrial-revolution world.

This still leaves open the question whether or not the slower economic growth which led up to the industrial revolution had itself begun at some distinct point of past time before which the economy had been stagnant or had grown very slowly indeed. Charles Wilson, for example, argues convincingly that the turning-point in economic growth was in 1660 rather than in 1760, and was in mercantilism rather than *laissez-faire*; 'commercial enterprise, often closely allied with state power and aided by legislation and military or naval force, was changing the face of the old agrarian customary economy', preparing the way for industrialization.[1] Only detailed and accurate statistics could give certainty to this thesis. The statistics, such as they are, show certainly only that growth was proceeding already in 1700. This indicates that any turning-point must be dated from an earlier period, from 1660, as Charles Wilson suggests, or, even earlier, from 1540 when J. U. Nef reckons that the first great industrial expansion of England commenced.[2]

The second controversy is more concerned with the mechanics of growth. Was the base from which the industrialization of the eighteenth century proceeded broad or narrow? Did it begin with one industry, or in one region? Was there a leading sector?[3] Or rather, was the base economy-wide, change proceeding from many sectors? In so far as the industrial revolution has been explained by the expanding cotton industry of Lancashire spreading its beneficial influence throughout the economy, then the argument has been one of sectoral growth. In so far as the industrial revolution has been explained by changes in social attitudes or habits which encouraged growth – for example, from the growth of the Protestant ethic of individualism, or from an increase generally in the propensity

[1] Charles Wilson, *England's Apprenticeship, 1603–1763* (London, 1965), p. x.

[2] J. U. Nef, 'The Progress of Technology and the Growth of Large Scale Industry in Great Britain, 1540–1640', *The Economic History Review*, 1st series, V (1934).

[3] The leading-sector thesis is developed in W. W. Rostow's *The Process of Economic Growth* (Oxford, 1960), Chapter 11.

to save – then the argument has been one of general change affecting the whole of the economy. These views can be called respectively the leading-sector theory and the aggregate-growth theory of the industrial revolution. The leading-sector theory argues that one sector (or small number of sectors) acted as the growth point(s), stimulating development by backward and forward linkages in complementary activities.[1] The aggregate-growth theory argues that growth occurred across the whole economy (or large sectors of it), because of a change in some variable (or variables) with economy-wide effects.

Interestingly enough, because of a failure to conceptualize problems, the historians, although they have tended to argue one way or the other, have not realized clearly that these two views of the industrial revolution conflict. Nor has there been much awareness that an obvious parallel with the historical controversy is the modern economic controversy about the appropriate economic policy for stimulating growth in an underdeveloped economy;[2] whether or not growth is best stimulated by a growth sector (or sectors) in a process of *unbalanced* growth, or by planned growth in all sectors in a process of *balanced* growth.[3] Whether or not eighteenth-century growth was balanced or unbalanced, the historical problem remains of showing *how* impulses were transferred from growth sectors to other sectors of the economy, and *why* other sectors responded to those impulses. To the extent that growth is assumed to have been sectoral, induced from a leading sector, then the linkages of that sector with the rest of the

---

[1] Linkage effects are described in A. O. Hirschman, *The Strategy of Economic Development* (Yale, 1958). A linkage effect is the stimulation which investment in one industry provides for the expansion of other industries, either through 'input-provision' (backward linkages) or 'output-utilization' (forward linkages).

[2] However, see J. R. T. Hughes, 'Foreign Trade and Balanced Growth: the Historical Framework', *American Economic Review* (1959).

[3] There is a considerable literature on this controversy. See R. Nurkse, *Problems of Capital Formation in Underdeveloped Countries* (Oxford, 1953), and A. O. Hirschman, op. cit., for and against balanced growth. Balanced growth supporters argue that investment decisions are mutually reinforcing and that over-all supply creates its own demand; unbalanced growth supporters argue that the poverty of underdeveloped countries makes the creation of strategic imbalances the only route to growth. I am indebted to Prof. D. Whitehead for ideas about balanced growth and the industrial revolution.

economy, and the responsiveness of the rest of the economy, are both assumed away; growth occurred, so there must have been both strong linkages and also a responsive economy. This has led to a tendency to neglect the characteristics of the economy which made it respond successfully to pressures from growth sectors.

And, since economists have assumed explicitly, and historians implicitly, that the growth of the industrial economies of Western Europe, including England, was achieved by a process of unbalanced growth, a key problem in the analysis of the industrial revolution has been neglected. More plausibly, however, one would have expected linkages in the pre-industrial-revolution economy not to have been strong: the economy was more self-sufficient, with a smaller export sector; the economy was more regionalized with local rather than national markets; industries tended also to depend more on local raw materials; there was little labour mobility; the producer goods industry was small. Moreover, if one considers the cotton industry as the leading sector of the industrial revolution, that industry's relatively weak linkages with the economy (in its demand for raw materials and in the disposal of its final product, for example) have to be explained away.

Because of the nature of the economy before the industrial revolution, and because of the character of the so-called leading-sectors of the industrial revolution, it is certain that the industrial revolution was the result of general growth, of a wide, if weak, response to a large number of sectoral growth points. Two important phenomena which support this thesis were the widely based advances in technology and the widely spread increase in home demand.[1] Add to these the more efficient recruitment of savings which led to an increase in capital formation, and the changes taking place in attitudes towards work, wealth, risk, and enterprise, and the case for a balanced growth interpretation of the industrial revolution is indisputable.

The third controversy is also concerned with process, and discusses the propositions that there were either *prerequisites*

[1] These phenomena are spelled out in more detail below, in Chapter 3.

for, or *stages of growth* leading up to, the industrial revolution.[1] Here again the theories of W. W. Rostow have been influential: in his article on 'the take-off', Rostow defined some necessary prerequisites for the take-off, and in his book on 'the stages of economic growth', the take-off becomes one of the stages. But the theory of stages did not originate with Rostow; it was formulated quite clearly in 1893 by the German economist, Carl Bücher, in his book *Industrial Evolution*.[2]

The stage theory usually goes like this: the industrial revolution (stage 4) was preceded by stage one, the commercial revolution (beginning in the seventeenth century), by stage 2, the agricultural revolution (beginning in the early eighteenth century) and by stage 3, the transport revolution (of the second half of the eighteenth century). The implication is that each revolution was preceded by one or more necessary prior revolutions, and that the cumulative effect of the commercial, agricultural, and transport revolutions was to produce the industrial revolution. The greatest problems of the stages analysis are, first, the difficulty of rigorously defining the characteristics of each stage; second, of dating the transition from stage to stage; and third, of describing the mechanism whereby the transition from stage to stage is achieved. The mechanism of growth for the industrial revolution, in spite of much writing about prior revolutions, remains obscure.[3] Moreover, implicit in the stages theory of growth is a sectoral thesis, of leadership in turn by important sectors with, necessarily, strong linkages with the sectors preceding and succeeding. Such serial linkages have not been established by research, and, indeed, are difficult to identify and separate chronologically. Changes in commerce, agriculture,

---

[1] However, as A. K. Cairncross points out, 'pre-conditions' or 'prerequisites' are 'a logical rather than a chronological concept', and presumably, unlike stages, need not necessarily precede the industrial revolution ('the take-off'). *Factors in Economic Development*, op. cit., p. 140.

[2] Carl Bücher, *Industrial Evolution*, trans. S. M. Wickett (New York, 1912).

[3] Nevertheless, this type of analysis still remains popular. M. W. Flinn in his *The Origins of the Industrial Revolution* sets out four prerequisites of the industrial revolution (improvements in agriculture, transport, the monetary and educational systems), and Phyllis Deane in *The First Industrial Revolution* also implies allegiance to a stages theory involving demography, agriculture, commerce, and transport.

transport, and industry were intimately related in an ongoing process of growth in which simultaneous interdependence was the main characteristic.

We must agree with A. Gerschenkron in rejecting the idea of 'uniform prerequisites of industrial development'.[1] Industrial development generally does not proceed in *a certain way*, in discrete stages. The disguised sectoral interpretation of the industrial revolution, in the form of a stages theory, does little more than suggest some important variables of growth, and give some idea of the chronology of growth; it does not explain growth. In particular, such an approach fails, as A. K. Cairncross points out, 'to distinguish between the preconditions and the conditions of economic growth'.[2] The revolutions in commerce, agriculture, and transport were, in no senses, completed before the industrial revolution; indeed, the greatest advances, quantitatively and in influence, took place with industrialization. Canals and turnip husbandry *may* have preceded industrialization; railways and high farming were certainly part of industrialization.

V

A detailed consideration of the roles of capital formation, increasing foreign trade, improving technology, and changing values is found in two of the chapters below.[3] Here the arguments are considered only briefly. On capital accumulation, the crucial fact is that there was at no time in the eighteenth century a marked rise in the rate of investment out of national income. Foreign trade, although expanding, absorbed insufficient a proportion of national output to have been more than a contributing factor to growth. Improving technology can be associated directly with rising output, but this is to say no more than that better machines and organization raised productivity;

---

[1] A. Gerschenkron, *Economic Backwardness in Historical Perspective* (Harvard University Press, 1962), Chapter 2.

[2] *Factors in Economic Development*, op. cit., p. 140.

[3] Chapters 3 and 7 by R. M. Hartwell and F. Crouzet.

it does not explain the sources of invention. Similarly with changing values; values did change and these were reflected in changing institutions (for example, greater commercial freedom), but the great doubt remains that values changed more as a rationalization for changing structure, a response to changing economic conditions, than the reverse.

P. Deane and W. A. Cole reckon that net capital formation was about 5 per cent of the national income in 1688, no more than 6 per cent in 1780, and perhaps 7 per cent by 1800.[1] The figures are not high; nor are they surprising when compared with the comparatively modest accumulation of modern developed economies. In the relatively poorer economy of the eighteenth century, the saving capacity was lower and capital accumulation proportionately less. It is perhaps paradoxical to inquire, therefore, whether low savings were a serious constraint to eighteenth-century growth, rather than, as is more conventionally supposed, whether there was a substantial increase in the savings rate which encouraged growth. A dramatic change in the savings rate, such as W. W. Rostow posits for his 'take-off', is certainly out of the question: there is no discernible institutional, political, economic, or social turning-point in the eighteenth century beyond which people quickly doubled their savings.[2] On the other hand, there is no convincing evidence that the lack of savings held back growth. England was not a poor country, even in 1700. The importance of savings was understood; there were men of all ranks increasingly willing and able to save. There were, moreover, plenty of opportunities for profitable investment, and increasingly in manufactures and finance, as well as in agriculture and trade. And entrepreneurs were not inhibited by many of the grave obstacles to growth which so frustrate the entrepreneur in a modern underdeveloped economy; for example, there was neither severe population pressure nor inadequate supplies of essential raw materials. And there was an improving and grow-

[1] *British Economic Growth*, op. cit., p. 263.
[2] Rostow argues for a quick increase in net investment from 5 per cent to 10 or 12 per cent of national income as the decisive factor causing economic growth. This is the view also of A. Lewis.

ing capital market which brought together savers and investor-entrepreneurs.[1]

A significant change, as regards productivity, was in the structure of the nation's accumulated capital: industrial capital was increasing proportionately to capital in land. In the process of capital formation, with high investment in construction and inventories, that part which embodied technical progress must have been small, even though it was increasing. With continuous technical progress, however, more new capital and an increasing proportion of replacement capital embodied new techniques; the capital stock was thus continually improved so that at any time during the eighteenth century the inherited capital stock was more efficient than at any previous time. It was this sort of process, which produced a more efficient rather than a proportionately larger capital stock, that explains the gradual rise in output which led up to the industrial revolution. The importance of technical change rather than capital formation for growth has been underlined by modern economic studies of empirical production functions which show that large increases in output, both in an economy and in sectors of an economy, relative to labour and capital inputs, involve little or no change in labour–capital ratios.[2] This was also so in the eighteenth century.

On the bases of belief, and on the relation between belief and action, especially economic action, there are large generalizations but insufficient research. The generalizations are well known: English Protestantism encouraged economic growth;[3] the Whig Revolution of 1688 was a triumph for individual liberty, and greatly increased the political influence, and greatly enhanced the social prestige, of the commercial and industrial classes, whose rational economic values became more generally

[1] See Charles Wilson, *England's Apprenticeship*, op. cit., Chapters 10 and 15, for an excellent account of financial developments after 1660 up to 1750. Also, P. G. M. Dickson, *The Financial Revolution in England. A Study in the Development of Public Credit 1688–1756* (London, 1967).

[2] See S. Fabricant, *Basic Facts on Productivity Change*, National Bureau of Economic Research, Occasional Paper 63 (New York, 1958).

[3] The most famous exposition in English of this thesis was by R. H. Tawney in *Religion and the Rise of Capitalism* (London, 1926).

acceptable;[1] the growth of science, and the increasing use of quantitative measurement for social facts ('Political Arithmetic'), encouraged rationality in economic life;[2] the development of 'the political theory of possessive individualism', summed up in the writings of John Locke, enshrined property rights by law and ensured the integrity of individual enterprise by giving the control of civil society to men of property.[3] Of these generalizations only the first has been seriously challenged,[4] but the others have yet to be translated into indexes of 'increasing commercialization', 'increasing economic rationality', and 'increasing social mobility', and all leave open the possibility that changing ideas, whether about science or politics, were responses to, as much as initiators of, economic growth.

The problem of economic growth, however, is obviously not just an economic one. As A. K. Cairncross has pointed out: 'Development may be impossible without building the physical apparatus of advanced countries; but it is still more impossible if it does not take place in the minds of the men who build.'[5] The human attributes which economic growth requires – 'knowledge and experience, skill and self-discipline, the power to take a long view, willingness to be guided by reason and observation, readiness to look for new and better things, responsiveness to opportunity and adaptability to change'[6] – are basically the products of upbringing and education. On the development of the social environment which produced these necessary attributes we know precious little, although some studies of 'motivational analysis' are now suggesting directions

---

[1] This was long ago recognized by Lecky: 'The political influence of the industrial and moneyed classes was greatly increased by the Revolution', *History of England in the Eighteenth Century* (London, 1878–92), Vol. I, p. 201.

[2] See G. N. Clark, *Science and Social Welfare in the Age of Newton* (Oxford University Press, 2nd edn, 1949); W. Letwin, *The Origins of Scientific Economics* (London, 1963).

[3] This theme is developed brilliantly by C. B. Macpherson in his *The Political Theory of Possessive Individualism: Hobbes to Locke* (Oxford University Press, 1962).

[4] See K. Samuelsson, *Religion and Economic Action* (London, 1961), for a summary and criticism of the literature on 'religion and the rise of capitalism'.

[5] *Factors in Economic Development*, op. cit., p. 31.

[6] Ibid.

which research could take.[1] For example, it is argued by E. E. Hagan that 'there can be no increase in innovational activity in a society without change in personality between generations, resulting from change in childhood environment'.[2] This generalization emphasizes relatively short-term changes. It is important to remember, also, that it was European civilization through many centuries of social and intellectual change which provided the matrix of modern economic growth. No non-European society, *except* Japan, has yet had successful economic growth, and this suggests that whatever shorter-term impulses triggered off the industrial revolution in England, industrialization generally was the product of a European civilization long in the making. We can conclude only that European and English history must be re-examined with the problems of economic growth and social change firmly in mind, so that the nature of social change can itself be better understood and so that the role of social change can be integrated into our explanations of economic growth.

At the simplest level of explanation, all economic change is the result of two factors: new knowledge (particularly, but not exclusively, technical knowledge), and the effective use in the production of goods and services of that knowledge.[3] There are, obviously, four problems for investigation: the sources of new knowledge, the means of communication of new knowledge, the motivation for the application of that knowledge, and the effectiveness of society and economy in using that knowledge (in realizing its potential and in being flexible enough to respond effectively). Assuming the existence of new knowledge, the problem is that of examining the economy's *elasticity of response*, and of analysing the *response mechanism*

[1] See *Social Theory and Economic Change*, T. Burns and S. B. Saul (eds.) (London 1967), especially the chapters by M. W. Flinn and E. E. Hagan, for the use of social theory to explain economic change in the eighteenth century.

[2] Ibid., p. 35. See also his book, *On the Theory of Social Change* (London, 1964), and *The Achieving Society* (Princeton, 1961) by D. D. McClelland.

[3] S. Kuznets (*Economic Growth and Structure*, op. cit., pp. 83–4) argues that, 'the sustained growth of population and product was made possible by the increasing stock of tested knowledge'; and 'one might define modern economic growth as the spread of a system of production . . . based upon the increased application of science, that is, an organised system of tested knowledge'.

C

whereby the new knowledge is actually embodied in a new production method, and the *diffusion process* whereby change at one point is transferred to other parts of the economy. On the origins of knowledge itself the traditional view is that new knowledge – invention – is exogenously determined, as far as the economy is concerned, but that the application of new knowledge – innovation – is economically motivated.[1] Certainly innovation is always restrained by economic factors – by resource availability and demand potential – but surely, also, invention is in varying degrees stimulated or restrained by market forces? Invention, indeed, is the product of individual insight, of the growth rate of knowledge, and of social and economic incentives. The growth of knowledge sets limits to the possibilities of invention; the pressures of the market provide tangible incentives or disincentives to inventive effort. The growth of science had reached a point by 1700 where even more complicated machines than the steam engine were possible; the great inventors of the eighteenth century were almost invariably motivated by practical problems of production, and they sought wealth in inventive effort.[2]

The response of the economy to invention was a matter of economic and social maturity, of having the right human and physical resources and the possibility of combining them in profitable enterprise. Only a reasonably developed economy could profit from invention which needed, for successful application, at least, a skilled labour force, energetic entrepreneurs, and a potential market for the goods of the technically reformed industry. The characteristics of poor and underdeveloped economies have been listed frequently by the economist,[3] but rarely by the historian, even though England of the eighteenth century has often been described as underdeveloped. To the economist, underdevelopment means the following: a

[1] See S. C. Gilfillan, 'Invention as a Factor in Economic History', *Journal of Economic History*, v, Supplement (1945).

[2] See M. Blaug, 'A Survey of the Theory of Process-Innovations', *Economica*, February 1963.

[3] See B. Higgins, *Economic Development. Problems, Principles and Policies* (London, 1959), pp. 6–21; and H. Leibenstein, *Economic Backwardness and Economic Growth* (New York, 1957), pp. 40–1.

very high proportion of the population (more than two-thirds) in agriculture; incomes so low that most income is spent on food and necessities, savings are small, and there is little capital per head; an economically backward population (backward in education, skills, and attitudes) with a tendency to grow faster than output; poorly developed markets with a low volume of *per capita* trade, the result of poor communications and inadequate credit facilities; a low level of agrarian techniques and low yields per acre, and crude technology in industry. With both incomes and savings low, the economy is caught in a vicious circle in which insufficient demand and investment are incapable of stimulating growth.

On these criteria England in the century before the industrial revolution was not underdeveloped: forty per cent of the population was in agriculture, and the proportion was declining; there was no population pressure and the population was relatively sophisticated economically; resources were underdeveloped but plentiful, and the output of coal had been increasing continuously since the sixteenth century; there was already a large capital stock and an advanced technology; wages were above subsistence, and there was considerable saving; there were large towns and an industrial sector with a substantial export trade; there were well-developed financial and commercial institutions; there were schools and universities and learned societies; there was a flourishing book-publishing industry. This was no underdeveloped economy; there was already a vast 'heritage of improvement'; the 'imbecile institutions of society', as T. V. Veblen called them, had been modified sufficiently to accept economic progress; social values had changed to the point where there was a growing appreciation of factories (more income) as well as of country houses (a pleasant way of life); the responsiveness of the economy was high because the market mechanism worked well. Briefly the economy before the industrial revolution was already well advanced, and it was experiencing growth.

VI

When did the growth that culminated in the industrial revolution begin? Searching back through the two centuries of English history which preceded the revolution, the Restoration marks the obvious change of trend. Not only did it follow half a century of depression, but it saw the beginnings of a notable advance in trade, of progress in agriculture and industry, and of the construction of an effective apparatus of government regulation to stimulate national prosperity. In agriculture, advances in husbandry technique and improvements in agrarian organization boosted the supply of food and raw materials, improved agricultural incomes, and expanded the market for industrial goods.[1] The crucial innovations were in the supply of fodder crops, inspired by a swing in the ratio of cereal–livestock prices in favour of livestock; this led to further colonization and to the development of mixed farming. The rise in livestock prices came partly from an increasing demand for meat, and partly from an increasing demand from industry for industrial raw materials like wool and leather. In industry, there were significant changes in the pattern of manufactures: the rise of new industries which hitherto had been confined to the home (for example, brewing and soap making), the expansion and diversification of the textile industry (for example, into cottons), the growth of coal mining (for industrial and domestic purposes), and the general expansion of other mining (for example, in tin, copper, and salt mining).[2] Two characteristics distinguished the industrial change of this period from that which preceded it: an increasingly complicated technology (for example, as used by the instrument makers) and a tendency towards geographical concentration (for example, the woollen industry of Yorkshire). Already the industrial map of nineteenth-century England was taking shape in the seventeenth. It is difficult to say much about the domestic market after 1660, but foreign trade for the next half century prospered, England becoming a

---

[1] See E. L. Jones, *Agriculture and Economic Growth in England, 1650–1815*, in this series.

[2] See Charles Wilson, *England's Apprenticeship*, op. cit., Chapter 9.

world entrepôt, with a growing merchant marine, expanding port facilities, and an increasing and wealthy community of merchants.[1] Equally important were the appearance of the long-term mortgage, the fall in the rate of interest, and the foundation of the Bank of England and a national debt.[2]

Because of these changes Charles Wilson claims that, 'The Restoration has a better claim than most dates to be regarded as the economic exit from medievalism,' and that the mercantile system was 'the necessary matrix within which the infant economy had to be coaxed into growth'.[3] Poverty, the economists believe, tends to be self-perpetuating, while growth also tends to generate its own momentum, once it has commenced. The problem is to get started, and for this some decisive change in the context of customary enterprise *may* be necessary. Government policy clearly changed, but the story of economic growth was less dramatic. After 1660 a large number of small growth points of increasing employment outside of agriculture absorbed an increasing proportion of the agricultural under-employed into productive enterprise, both in industry and in commerce. The expansion of the non-agricultural sector had already progressed far when Gregory King made his estimate of 'the Comparative Strength of Great Britain' in 1696, showing that only 40 per cent of the national product came from agriculture.

In the eighteenth century these trends continued: more labour was more fully employed; more resources were available and more were switched to higher productivity uses; and the human and physical capital stock were both increased and improved. In agriculture acreage was extended, and further changes in husbandry and organization resulted in a striking expansion of output. Two other agricultural phenomena were highly important: the twenty years of good harvests after 1730 which kept agricultural prices low, forced structural change within agriculture, and boosted purchasing power at a time

[1] R. Davis, 'English Foreign Trade 1660–1700', *The Economic History Review*, 2nd series, VII, No. 2 (1954).
[2] H. J. Habakkuk, 'The Price of Land in England, 1500–1700', *Wirtschaft, Geschichte und Wirtschaftsgeschichte*, W. Abel and others (eds.) (Stuttgart, 1966).
[3] *England's Apprenticeship*, op. cit., pp. 236, 237.

when food prices dominated wages; the drying up of the land market which forced up the price of land, making it essential for farmers to be price-conscious, and encouraging those who customarily invested in land to consider alternative investment. A conventional price for land was replaced by a market price; land became another good to be purchased rationally. Undoubtedly the low food prices before 1750 occurred at a critical point of development. The precarious balance of food supplies and population, which in previous ages had periodically tipped against population to produce famines and plagues, was by 1730 firmly weighted in favour of increasing numbers. Then came an exogenous increase in food supplies, a bounty of nature which allowed more people to survive and increased real incomes by lowering the price of the main items of expenditure in low-income budgets.

The relationship of population growth to economic growth is both interesting and complex: increasing population means an increase in one factor of production; over history, population growth has undoubtedly been an important source of increasing output, because, until recently, of the comparative unimportance of capital, and because also of labour's ability, in combination with simple tools and traditional methods to increase production. In the eighteenth century before 1750 more food allowed a greater population and a greater output; cheaper food allowed an increase and diversification of demand, both for domestic manufactures and for colonial products (like tea and sugar). The 1740s, for these reasons, was a decade of quickening growth, with increasing investment in manufacturing and foreign trade, and consequent income and employment generation in the non-agricultural sectors of the economy.

At the next stage of development, when population was increasing more rapidly, the translation of population growth into effective demand provided the market opportunities for continued investment. The rise of demand is seen most clearly in the rising consumption of imported groceries, but it can be seen also in the broadening range of consumer goods, the substitution of new and better articles for older and cruder ones (for example, in pottery), and in the improvement of the market, for example in the establishment of the retail shop as a method of distribution. 'The emergence of the provincial shop from the welter of markets, fairs and hawkers' was part of the process of improving the market.[1] So also was the improvement of roads and rivers, and the building of canals. In so far as the market was limited by high transport costs and small towns, the canal building and urbanization of the second half of the eighteenth century were most important. In so far as the market was limited by low incomes, the increase of wages on the one hand,[2] and the lowering of the costs of production of manufactured goods on the other, were also important. As Heaton points out, below: 'The story is not one of insistent demand compelling changes in productive methods; it is rather one in which changed methods and lower production costs resulted in a commodity which created a big new demand'. And this occurred, again as Heaton underlines, in 'the largest free-trade area in the world', in a now well-established national market not bedevilled with those internal trade barriers which so frustrated much trade on the Continent. For the servicing of this market the commercial population of England had grown 'both relatively and absolutely during the century preceding the Industrial Revolution'.[3] This community of merchants also serviced an external trade which continued to grow, both in America and in Europe. If the period before 1760 had seen greatest expansion in colonial trade, the fastest growing sector after 1780 was in Europe. Foreign trade, however, was unstable and still relatively small. As M. W. Flinn argues: 'the fact remains that for most individual industries, and certainly for all industries put together, home demand predominated, and was therefore able to exercise a more decisive influence on output'.[4]

From mid-century there was increasing investment in agri-

---

[1] A. H. John, 'Aspects of English Economic Growth in the First Half of the Eighteenth Century', *Essays in Economic History*, Vol. 2, E. M. Carus-Wilson (ed.) (London, 1962), p. 369.

[2] As demonstrated by E. W. Gilboy in *Wages in Eighteenth Century England* (Harvard University Press, 1934).

[3] R. B. Westerfield, *Middlemen in English Business, 1660–1760* (Yale University Press, 1915), p. 412.

[4] *Origins of the Industrial Revolution*, op. cit., p. 62.

culture (the result of the increasing price of food after 1750, because of population pressure and poorer harvests), in communications (to lower costs and enlarge markets), and in industry (to meet the increasing demands of a more affluent and larger population). More land was brought into cultivation and more raw materials were brought into industrial production; there was rising productivity in industry because of technical change. Growth was prompted by the increasing supply of factors, by the changing technology and by the increasing demand. Investment plus invention increased productivity in industry, created further employment and tended to push up wages. However, since interest rates remained low, and wages rose only slowly, there was neither a capital nor labour shortage to inhibit enterprise. Although demand remained buoyant, the costs of enterprise remained relatively low, and investment was encouraged. The turning-point came in the eighties, when the mounting pressure of demand, both real and potential, created pressures on industry to further increase productivity. This resulted in a series of notable technical breakthroughs which so reduced the price of industrial goods that not only was domestic demand greatly increased, but English goods were cheap enough also to invade, even over tariff and transport barriers, the mass market of Europe. The industrial revolution had begun.

VII

The articles which follow have been chosen both to summarize a large literature about the industrial revolution, and also to illustrate certain important themes in that literature. Heaton's essay, published in 1933, is a descriptive survey-article by an historian, going well beyond Britain geographically and well beyond 1800 chronologically, and is still the best short general article on the industrial revolution. It is 'pre-growth-conscious' in character, gives a typical listing of causes, and although Heaton favours a technological interpretation of growth, he gives appropriate weighting to a wide range of factors (trade expansion, improving commercial and financial structure, changing industrial organization, etc.). Heaton also has a theory of growth, as can be seen in his discussion of what he calls 'spearheads of the technological advance' (i.e. 'leading sectors') and of the 'roughly similar course' of industrialization taken by different countries (i.e. 'stages of growth'). The article also has a discussion, later developed by J. U. Nef[1] and F. Crouzet (in this volume), about the differing economic histories of France and England in the eighteenth century. Hartwell's article is also a survey article, from the point of view, however, of an economist of growth; it summarizes and criticizes the theories of the historians about the industrial revolution; it is scarcely less charitable to the economists' attempts to explain growth; it outlines the problems to be solved but offers no solution. Deane's article shows how contemporary estimates of national income and wealth can be used to give a clear picture of the changing overall structure of the English economy between the end of the seventeenth and the beginning of the nineteenth centuries, the crucial period of growth; in particular, it quantifies the increasing importance of manufacturing and commerce as employers and producers of wealth, and, also, the increase in output which resulted from transferring resources from agriculture to industry and services. Wrigley illustrates the supply side of the industrial revolution, the increasing inputs of industrial raw materials (especially coal) which were 'the *sine qua non* of sustained economic growth'. Too often industrial revolution studies have ignored or under-emphasized the great increase in productive factors (land, labour, raw materials) which was responsible for so much of the increase in total output. Wrigley redresses this failure, and, in particular, underlines the importance for industrialization of increasing coal supplies, and argues that the contrast in coal production in the eighteenth century between England and the economies of continental Europe is both the cause and the measure of their differing economic growth. With Gilboy, we move from supply to demand, for as Gilboy emphasizes, 'without a large and growing demand ready and willing to absorb its products as fast as they are produced', the factory system could

[1] *The Industrial Revolution Reconsidered*, op. cit.

not have functioned. This original and provocative essay of 1932 was written before the Keynesian emphasis on demand, and demonstrates that 'changing consumption standards' in England were necessary for the industrial revolution to have occurred. More attention to this article[1] would certainly have made it more difficult for the pessimists in the debate on the standard of living; its neglect can best be explained by the obscurity of its place of publication, embedded in a *Festschrift*. Crouzet takes up the difficult problem of explaining why France did not have an industrial revolution in the eighteenth century, by a close comparison of the economic histories of France and England in the seventeenth and eighteenth centuries. Crouzet builds up an intriguing picture of small but cumulative differences between the two economies which finally, in the case of England, resulted in the economy reaching a point where supply could not meet demand without 'a technological breakthrough'. According to Crouzet both countries were proceeding inevitably in the same direction; but England reached a 'critical mass' position before France, and this set in motion a chain reaction, which was the industrial revolution.

[1] See C. R. Fay, *English Economic History mainly since 1700* (Cambridge, 1940), for a rare and early discussion of the importance of demand.

2 Industrial Revolution

H. HEATON

[This article was first published in the *Encyclopaedia of the Social Sciences*, Vol. VIII (1933).]

Industrial revolution is the name given to those economic and technological developments which gathering strength and speed during the eighteenth century produced modern industrialism.

As a label it is admittedly unsatisfactory. One writer calls it 'an unhappily chosen epithet for a singularly constructive epoch' (Beales); another doubts whether the term, 'though useful enough when it was first adopted, has not by this time served its turn' (Unwin); Lipson occasionally puts it in inverted commas. The chief objection is to the word revolution. Yet that use goes back to the period to which it is applied. Yarn-making machines, coke-smelted iron, Watt's engine and Wedgwood's ceramic triumphs were described by contemporaries as 'great and extraordinary', 'most wonderful'; their effects must be 'beyond the power of calculation'. The steam engine would 'produce great changes in the appearance of the civilized world'; and 'a revolution is making', said Arthur Young in 1788 when he saw the textile machines spread from the cotton to the woollen industry. Frenchmen after 1789 naturally used the word even more freely in reference to changes in technique, organization, and commercial policy; and it became part of the socialistic vocabulary. Blanqui in 1837 declared that by the revolution industrial conditions in England had been more profoundly transformed than at any period since the beginnings of social life. Engels used the word in 1845, and the Marxian thesis was that the technological revolution had transformed the economic and social structure and would do the same to political and intellectual life. Toynbee knew Marx'

Capital, had studied the German socialist movement and was undoubtedly influenced thereby in his use and understanding of the term he put into academic circulation. Mill and Jevons also spoke of revolution; and in 1852 Michael Angelo Garvey, an English barrister, published a little volume called *The Silent Revolution*, which dealt with the effects of steam transportation and the telegraph on 'the condition of mankind'.

To Toynbee the use of the word seemed entirely justified. He envisaged a peaceful eve followed by a stormy dawn. Prior to 1760 the 'old industrial system obtained'; industry was in the hands of small independent master manufacturers who combined farming and industry, employed a journeyman or two and trained an apprentice. Between master and man was a 'warm attachment'; the employee was the 'cherished dependent'. The class of capitalist employers was 'as yet in its infancy'; there was some putting out of materials by merchants to be worked up in the operative's home, and a few large factories were in existence. But small-scale organization predominated, and the gulf between employer and wage-earner was narrow. Over this 'quiet world' of 'scarcely perceptible movement', this 'slowly dissolving framework of medieval industrial life', hung the comprehensive code of state regulation of production, trade, and distribution. Internal free trade had come in Great Britain, but foreign and colonial trade were fettered and free movement or enterprise was checked.

This old order 'was suddenly broken in pieces by the mighty blows of the steam engine and the power loom', the spinning machines, the improved roads, the expansion of domestic and foreign trade and the *Wealth of Nations*. The 'two men who did most to bring [the revolution] about were Adam Smith and James Watt'; aided by the other inventors, they 'destroyed the old world and built a new one'. A period of 'economic revolution and anarchy' resulted, in which productive methods changed, economic beliefs were revolutionized and the state swung over from regulation to *laissez-faire*. Population was 'torn up by the roots' and, like industry, was dragged 'from cottages in distant valleys into factories and cities', there to become a collection of hands, 'the living tool, of whom the employer knew less than he did of his steam engine'. Population grew rapidly in numbers, but the number engaged in agriculture declined both relatively and absolutely; the factory system became the 'all-prominent fact' in industry; overproduction and depressions – 'a phenomenon quite unknown before' – became normal parts of business life; landlords and manufacturers waxed rich, but the wage earner fared badly. True, he now had personal freedom, but war prices and the 'innumerable evils which prevailed in this age of confusion' made his sufferings acute and long. Eventually his lot improved, thanks to organized self-help, the repeal of the corn laws, and factory acts; but meanwhile he had been in the track of a social tornado, which had torn him from his old moorings and left him damaged in status and living standards.

Toynbee put the industrial revolution into the series of historical phases. Henceforth it was apparent that for any understanding of the nineteenth century one must take account of English economics as well as of French politics. The term became popular, and at least two recent writers have described post-war efforts towards rationalization and the changes resulting from the coming of electric power and new chemical processes as 'the New Industrial Revolution' (Meakin) and 'the Second Industrial Revolution' (Jevons). But economic historians use the phrase with increasing hesitation and many mental reservations. They dislike the suggestion that revolutions in any generally acceptable sense of that term happen in economic affairs. 'Sudden catastrophic change is inconsistent with the slow gradual process of economic evolution,' says Birnie; 'On the vast stage of economic history no sudden shift of scene takes place,' says Sée; while Lipson emerges from a study of the seventeenth and eighteenth centuries with the conclusion that there is 'no hiatus in economic development, but always a constant tide of progress and change, in which the old is blended almost imperceptibly with the new'.

The modern view springs from a fuller knowledge of the periods both before and after 1760 than was possible in Toynbee's day. It is now known that the revolution did not 'break' on an almost unchanging world of small-scale non-capitalistic units, that the speed of transformation was far from rapid, that the ground was not quickly captured and that a picture of the social and economic evils of the period from 1760 to 1850 is far from filling the whole canvas. In the first place, the notion of an 'eve' is blurred, if not blotted out, when it is discovered that the revolution had in 1760 'been in preparation for two centuries' (Unwin); that large-scale enterprise under capitalistic conditions existed from at least the sixteenth century; that the changes in technique were 'the completion of tendencies which had been significantly evident since Leonardo da Vinci' (Usher); and that the developments between 1760 and 1830 'did but carry farther, though on a far greater scale and with far greater rapidity, changes which had been proceeding long before' (Ashley). In the second place, the changes in productive methods depended on far more than a handful of inventions in Lancashire and Glasgow and with one or two exceptions took decades to work themselves out. The machines and engines raised as many problems as they solved – problems of metal supply, machine design, mechanical engineering, power transmission, and so on. Machine production could improve only as quickly as did the production of machines and the invention of refinements to make their operation more efficient. The nature of some processes or materials was such that change was long delayed; wool combing refused to yield to machinery until about 1850, and wool yarn was so frail that even in 1860 the power loom in a woollen mill could work no more quickly than did the hand loom. In some industries change resulted from chemical discoveries rather than mechanical invention; in others, such as pottery, advance depended upon the discovery, by countless experiments, of new bodies, glazes, methods of decoration, better understanding and control of kiln temperatures as well as upon easier access by road and canal to raw materials and markets. Mining had no revolution; its story was one of 'better methods . . . slowly forged from the painful experience of common men, and only gradually did a new idea or a new device spread from pit to pit or from one coalfield to another' (Ashton). Building, one of the biggest fields of employment, suffered no revolution in methods until cheap steel and concrete were available. Thus with the one exception of spinning and its preliminary processes there was no sudden breaking of old methods or organization by 'mighty blows'. Professor Clapham's survey of British industry between 1820 and 1850 is a study in slow motion. He finds that 'no single British industry had passed through a complete technical revolution before 1830' and reminds us that while the revolution had cut deep into the cotton industry by that date the Lancashire cotton operative was not the representative workman of the day. Even the typical town operative was 'very far indeed from being a person who performed for a self-made employer, in steaming air, with the aid of recently devised mechanism, operations which would have made his grandfather gape'. Thus it is not until well into the nineteenth century that one finds the economic transformation approaching a stage that can be described as complete. A revolution which continued for 150 years and had been in preparation for at least another 150 years may well seem to need a new label.

Yet despite all hesitation the term stands and no better one has been devised. For there is in the period which began about 1750 something different in tempo and temper from that of any earlier epoch. The long inventive effort comes to a head in increased productive power, capital increases its power and resourcefulness, economic freedom is gained, domestic and foreign trade expand, the nature of the soil begins to be understood, goods can be moved more rapidly in greater bulk at lower cost for longer distances, and there is at least a 'partial introduction of the methods of exact science in economic affairs' (Clapham). Any one of these things would have made a deep mark on the economic life of Europe; but when they came contemporaneously they interacted on one another and produced results which were far-reaching and fundamental. From this 'unprecedented social and economic development' (Unwin) the material appearance of England was changed 'more profoundly than at any other time since the epoch of the last geological changes' (Tawney).

The familiar question, 'Why did the changes come when and where they did?' is now best answered if the changes are regarded as the outcome of developments which had been under way since at least 1600. Those developments included a great expansion in the volume of domestic, colonial, and foreign trade; an improvement in commercial and financial structure; some growth of large-scale organization and production; some advances in industrial equipment; and some scientific discoveries capable of industrial application. British trade grew fitfully but substantially during the seventeenth and eighteenth centuries: the European demand expanded; the American colonists provided a growing market for textiles and hardware; the door into the Spanish possessions was forced wider open; while Africa, the West Indies, and the Orient provided good markets and profitable materials for carriage to Europe. Such statistics as exist show that exports from Great Britain doubled between 1720 and 1760 and again by 1795. Meanwhile the British population grew rapidly after, at latest, 1730, thanks chiefly to a declining death-rate. It lived on the largest free trade area in Europe; the wealth which flowed in from oversea trade gave its people a larger spending power and fund of capital; and some of the goods it imported stimulated natives to find ways of making these articles at home, e.g. cottons and pottery. The French story is somewhat similar. Export trade grew almost fivefold between 1715 and 1789 and was probably larger than that of Great Britain in the latter year. Shipowners and merchants flourished, and capital accumulated. Holland and Scandinavia also shared in the general trade expansion.

Economic organization improved during the seventeenth century. Banking and exchange facilities became more abundant and satisfactory, and joint stock companies were established for a large variety of purposes. Industries which served large or distant markets (textiles), which needed large sums of capital for equipment (mining, finishing trades), which worked on costly raw material (silk, precious metals) or which supplied customers who demanded long credit and were slow in paying their bills (London high-class tailoring, coach building) were passing into the hands of large entrepreneurs. Sometimes these men were big industrialists who had risen from small beginnings; but often they were merchants who established control over the production of the wares they sold. The merchant had capital or knew where to get it; he could afford to buy raw materials in bulk; he knew the needs of the market and he could allow long credit. He therefore sometimes gave orders to independent master manufacturers instead of buying what was offered in the open market; he supplied working capital to the mines from which he obtained his coal; but in some industries he took control. He bought raw materials and put them out to be processed by domestic workers; he supplied patterns and specifications and possibly the tools and equipment as well; while the final processes whether of finishing or assembling might be done in his own workshop. Independent master manufacturers still existed, who worked aided by the members of their family, journeymen, and apprentices, and sold their wares in fairs or local markets; such men could be found in the urban handicrafts catering for purely local needs and in the woollen districts of Yorkshire. But in the great staple industries – especially textiles – of France, the Low Countries, and England the merchant was gaining control and sometimes counted his dependents by the hundred or even the thousand. At times the economies of supervision, discipline and time saving were realized by gathering many of these workers under one roof; while in mining, brewing, soap-making, smelting, shipbuilding, tanning, and the finishing trades large groups of men had to work together by reason of the very nature of their work or of the equipment they used. Sometimes these groups worked under full factory conditions at machinery driven by power. Polhem's factory set up in Sweden about 1700 was remarkable for its use of machinery, water power, division of labour, and mass production methods.

The sixteenth and seventeenth centuries also witnessed some advance in industrial equipment and scientific knowledge. Leonardo da Vinci's notebooks contain sketches of a spinning machine, a power loom, roller bearings, universal joints, gears, lathes, drills, rollers for shaping iron, coin presses, turbines, steam cannon, and other things, but no one can tell how far they depict contemporary equipment or are the product of his fertile imagination. The stocking frame, invented about

D

1589, was said to contain over two thousand parts; and cloth finishing machines caused much controversy in the same century. Glassmaking, tinning, gold and silver refining, were all improved after 1600; makers of clocks, jewellery, and instruments of precision obtained better equipment; a ribbon loom capable of weaving a dozen or more widths at once appeared in Danzig, then in Holland, and finally in England; the Dutch developed the wind sawmill and other devices for speedy production of ships; the French experimented with the 'draw loom', by which patterned cloths could more easily be woven; Polhem's factory was full of power-driven metal shears, slitting mills, rollers, and hammers; and a silk-throwing machine which had been known in Italy before 1300 was copied north of the Alps and reached England in 1718. The harnessing of water, wind, and animal power became more efficient, as did the use of gears, while the use of treadles seems to have spread. The work of the growing body of scientists on atmospheric pressure had by 1700 laid a foundation on which the steam engine could be built. True, the seventeenth century saw more technical problems than it was able to solve but it was far from being devoid of inventive inquisitive minds.

The motives which led to the technical progress of the eighteenth century were many and varied. Steam engines and coke fuel came as aids to men who were fighting a losing battle. Shallow deposits of coal, tin, and copper were being exhausted, yet existing pumps could not cope with the water which seeped into the lower levels; ruin was inevitable unless the pumping problem could be solved. Ironmasters were faced with vanishing charcoal supplies as the forests near iron deposits were cut down; they must find a new fuel or abandon their furnaces. Many inventions aimed at saving labour, at making possible the use of children for processes formerly done by adults and at overcoming a scarcity of skilled labour. The whole textile industry was hampered in its growth by the fact that a large number of workers was needed to prepare yarn for one weaver; a cotton loom used the yarn made by four or five spinners; a woollen weaver kept nine or ten people busy; while in the sail-cloth industry Arthur Young found twenty yarn makers to each weaver. Since much of the spinning was done by country dwellers, weavers were often idle in summer when the spinners went to gather the harvest. In making patterned cloths the silk weaver needed the aid of three women to raise or lower the warp threads prior to the passage of the shuttle. In the metal industries the cutting of cogwheels for watches and other implements was slow and unsatisfactory until a machine was designed which 'reduced the expense of workmanship to a trifle in comparison to what it was before and [brought] the work to such an exactness that no hand can imitate it' (Campbell). Watt, Roebuck, and Wedgwood all had great difficulty in finding tools and men capable of making goods exact in measurement: there was an error of three-eighths of an inch in a cylinder made for Watt. Wilkinson's boring machine was designed to make possible the production of cannon and cylinders which would be uniform in diameter.

Inventive ingenuity was also stimulated by the hope of monetary reward. Leonardo da Vinci had planned a needle-polishing machine which was to bring him the income of a Medici, and eighteenth-century opinion grew more tolerant toward the inventor's claim to compensation. Even when patent rights were challenged, it was agreed that the inventor should be rewarded by some gift from the state or from some organization set up to encourage invention. Kings and parliaments protected or rewarded innovators, and such bodies as the Society for the Encouragement of Arts, Manufactures and Commerce, established in London in 1754, offered premiums, medals, and prizes.

The spearheads of the technological advance in the eighteenth century were iron, cotton, and pottery, and it is no mere accident that this should be so. For these industries were virtually new to England and were free from vested interests and government control. More important still, they had two markets, one to be captured, the other to be created. They strove to capture existing demands which were already met by supplies from the Continent or the Orient; but in addition they saw the vast demand which would spring into being if they could offer cheap cottons, crockery, or iron. Wedgwood showed his grasp of the situation when he established a Useful Branch as well as an Ornamental Branch. In the latter he won a luxury market once served by Dutch, French, German, and Oriental potters; in the former he created a new demand among all sections from the middle class to the poor. Lancashire cotton goods ousted oriental produce from the European, African, and plantation markets and eventually invaded the Orient itself; they stole some ground from the linen and woollen producers; but the total was insignificant when compared with the new demand for more clothing and for domestic decoration which the cheap fabrics created. The story is not one of insistent demand compelling changes in productive methods; it is rather one in which changed methods and lower production costs resulted in a commodity which created a new big demand.

These many stimuli to industrial change were at work in both France and Britain all through the eighteenth century. In each country invention and imitation were active, and the search for new ideas was made abroad as well as at home. England had welcomed the Huguenots after 1685; Lombe had copied the silk machine from Italy in 1718 and become a big factory owner; London paper makers strove eagerly to learn the secret of French, Dutch, and Italian superiority; London calico printers imitated the methods practised in Hamburg; while tin-plate makers set up rolling mills of Swedish design. The English countryside was sprinkled with methods, rotations, crops, and implements picked up by English gentlemen during their 'grand tour'; and such publications as the *Annual Register* and the *Gentleman's Magazine* gave space to descriptions of industrial and agricultural innovations. If one dare talk of 'the spirit of the Age', that spirit in the mid-century was certainly a powerful stimulant to interest in and search for new and better methods. Of that spirit nearly all sections of society were drinking.

Of the outcome of this enthusiasm no detailed account can be given here. The great inventors and discoverers whose names are known often built on foundations laid by scores of obscure men; their work was frequently an improvement or refinement upon that of others and in turn needed still further improvement before it became really satisfactory. Crompton's mule was, as its name suggests, at least a crossbred and did not do its best work until it was made self-acting nearly fifty years later. Watt's engine was originally only an improvement on that designed by Newcomen sixty years before, and until it obtained a crank action was little more than a somewhat more economical pump than its predecessor. Some men went searching on wrong tracks, and their chief contribution was that of warning others not to seek solutions in those directions. Cartwright's loom, for instance, seems to have been almost worthless. In the gallery of inventors some canvases are too large, some should not be there at all and many deserving ones have not yet been painted, much less hung.

By 1789 it was becoming apparent on both sides of the English Channel that Britain was pulling ahead of its nearest rival in industrial and agricultural technique. Young boasted that France had no counterparts to Arkwright, Wedgwood, Darby, Wilkinson, or Boulton and those Frenchmen who opposed the Anglo-French commercial treaty of 1786 pointed to the advantages Britain enjoyed through its lead in equipment; its comparative freedom from state interference; its supplies of iron, coal, china clay, and water power; its access to raw materials; its abundant supplies of capital in London, Liverpool, and Glasgow; and the power which its industrialists and merchants wielded in political life. These assets did much to make Britain the workshop of the world during the next fifty years; the Napoleonic wars strengthened its grip on the seas and weakened France's access to raw materials and markets, while the demands of these wars strengthened the demand for mass production of many commodities, a demand which the British inventions were particularly fitted to meet. Meanwhile France, which had been eagerly copying the British cotton and iron equipment before 1789, fell back; and although there was some development in the production of cotton, iron, and sugar during the revolution and war it ended that period economically weaker, with foreign trade crippled, capital scarce, transport facilities disorganized, and many skilled workers killed. Not until about 1830 did French economic effort begin seriously the task of modernization, and even in 1850 there was little that deserved to be called an industrial revolution. Fuel and raw materials were insufficient; capital was scarce; facilities for industrial investment were scanty; and the Frenchman was wedded to individualism, agriculture, and small-scale enterprise. Alsace-Lorraine was lost before ways were found of turning its ore into steel. Hence nineteenth-century France fell behind its traditional rival; Holland had no resources on which to build up the new kind of industry; and of the two countries which were best fitted to follow the English lead only Belgium moved quickly; Germany remained almost stationary until 1850, if not later. It had to wait until the Zollverein and railroads overcame the obstacles to easy movement of persons and goods. In Italy industrialization was retarded by political disunity and later by lack of raw materials.

Great Britain was therefore left almost alone in developing the new technique and organization. France did contribute something to the common stock of invention and discovery – silk throwing machines, the Jacquard loom, the tubular boiler, the water turbine, chemical bleaching, a sewing machine, and other things. Germany gave attention to the relations between science and production; Justus von Liebig put agricultural chemistry on its feet in 1840; nearly a century before that date Margraaf had found there was sugar in beetroot; while in 1802 the Silesian Achard found a way of extracting it on a commercial scale and thus gave Europe a new industry. After 1800 the North American contribution began to be important, and by 1850 American machine tools and machine products were entering the European market. The keynote of the American development was mass production of standardized articles, each part of which was made by machinery designed for one task. Skilled labour was scarce; the frontier consumer wanted goods which were cheap, serviceable, or labour saving rather than polished, well finished, and long of life. The designing of special machines which could be attended and fed by unskilled workers therefore became the first manifestation of 'Yankee ingenuity'; these machines produced parts which were of standard sizes and which could therefore be assembled quickly by the same kind of labour. From the making of muskets and revolvers this method of production spread to that of clocks, woodwork, sewing machines, harvesters, locks, and the like. English observers in the 1850s marvelled at the 'fearless and masterly manner' in which 'correct principles' were applied by American engineers. Still the crucial developments which led to production by power-driven machines did take place chiefly on British soil; it was there that the new factories, metallurgical plants, big coal mines, engineering shops, railroad, and steamship were worked out and the resulting social problems had first to be faced.

The workshop of the world exported industrial products to all parts; but soon its customers wished to import industrialism instead, and the encouragement of that importation has figured largely in the politics of most countries. The motive of this state fostering of industrialization was the belief that it was derogatory, disgraceful, and dangerous to remain a nation of farmers and handicraftsmen: dangerous because the handicrafts would be destroyed by the competition of imported machine products, because there would be no openings for those whose inclinations and talents were not rural and because the nation could not make its own war equipment; derogatory because the standards of the nineteenth century seemed to place the townsman on a higher plane than the rustic and the man who lived near a factory chimney above the hewer of wood, the shepherd or the cultivator; disgraceful because it was shameful to depend on other nations for the goods that one could and should make for oneself. If China, Japan, and India were to count in the eyes of the Western world they must Westernize their industrial equipment as well as their judicial and educational systems; if Canada, Australia, and even the United States were to emerge from colonial status or stature they must cut the ties that bound them to the factories of Lancashire, Yorkshire, and the Black Country; if new or reborn nations, such as Germany or Italy, were to make their unity or freedom real they must translate nationalism into factories, mines, banks, and statistics of industrial output; and if Russian communists wished to justify their faith and place in a hostile capitalistic world they must teach a nation of peasants how to make electricity, tractors, cloth, electric lamps, and cheap matches. Hence the political thought of nearly every nation has been obsessed with problems of protection and self-sufficiency and of nurturing industrial growth in face of the competition of more highly industrialized countries. Only the crack of doom will end the debate concerning the extent to which success, where it has come, has been the result of governmental action in granting tariffs, bounties, and the like, or has sprung from such other causes as abundant natural resources, improved transportation facilities, large home markets, and the inventive ability, organizing capacity, and industrious habits of the population.

In the New World there was some industrial revolution, but many industries came so late that they were able to begin operations on the modern plan. In the United States and to a slight degree in Australia and Canada there was some small-scale and domestic industry to be destroyed or superseded. Colonial America had its frontier household manufacture of cloth, clothes, furniture, and implements, its farm-house processing of land and animal products, its charcoal smelting of bog iron, its nail shops, town handicraftsmen; distilleries, potash plants, and shipyards. It had some putting out and some artisans who rambled round the countryside or worked in their own shops on materials belonging to their customers; and its flour, fulling, or sawmills often treated customers' grain, cloth, or lumber. But frontier conditions usually decided that the settler should rely on others only for those goods which he could not make for himself. Gradually most of these occupations passed into factories and workshops; there was a steady shedding of by-occupations by the farmer and a corresponding concentration on his main task. Improved roads, canals, and finally the railroad brought a wider area within reach of factory products and spinning wheel, churn, and candle mould became antiques. The interruption of Anglo-American relations during the revolution stimulated domestic production, while the period from 1807 to 1814 saw some adoption of machinery and factory organization; tariffs after 1815 helped the textile and iron industries over some of their difficulties with foreign competitors; the westward flow of population called for the production of settlers' effects at such inland points as Pittsburgh; the Erie Canal made it possible to process farm products at such centres as Buffalo and Rochester and to send them to eastern markets; the scarcity of labour stimulated the production of labour-saving farm implements and industrial machinery; while engines had to be designed and built suitable to American railroad conditions. But agriculture and commerce remained the chief interests until the Civil War; capital and enterprise found their richest rewards in the unoccupied areas of the west, in the production of staples for the seaboard or the European market, in land speculation, in supplying the stream of settlers, and in shipping. The really serious industrialization of the country did not set in until after 1860; by that time the methods and organization which seemed most suitable had already been worked out in New or old England and only needed to be adapted when adopted. The extension of industrialization to the south of the United States, slowly since 1890, with increasing rapidity since 1914, has again involved the imposition of known industrial techniques on an agricultural economic organization. Australia and Canada had little of the old order to sweep away; their industries could begin on the modern pattern. The South American countries are still predominantly agricultural, the only important traces of industrialization being the penetration of modern methods of finance, large-scale plantation organization and the spreading use of machinery in the extractive industries.

In the Near and Far East the machine technique has met a social organization far older and more stable than that which it superseded either in the countries of the New World or in Europe; but here too changes which may be called industrial revolutions have occurred or are in progress. The first of the oriental countries to feel the impact of industrialism was India. Conquest, railways, and foreign goods introduced the system. The dissolution of the old princedoms and their courts, followed by the rapid introduction of improved methods of transportation, and the prohibition of the importation of

Indian cottons and silks into England had gone far towards destroying the highly developed urban and village industries of India even before the products of English machines appeared upon the Indian market. Loss of older means of livelihood drove increasing numbers of artisans back upon agriculture, and meanwhile the relentless growth of population continued. By 1880 there were many observers who felt that the one solution of India's economic difficulties was the development of modern industries. The factory system appeared first in the 1850s with the building of cotton and jute mills. While the jute industry was developed almost entirely by English capital, the cotton mills were started by native Bombay merchants and the industry has remained largely in native hands. The growth of the cotton textile industry was slow until about 1880, when it began to expand rapidly. As has been true in most countries, machine spinning was at first far more important than weaving, large quantities of machine-spun yarn being used by Indian handloom weavers; even larger quantities were exported to China and for a time to Japan. This Chinese market was eventually lost to Japan, and after the World War Japan became a formidable competitor in the Indian market itself. Until 1914 India depended entirely upon imports for her machinery and industrial equipment. Early attempts to establish an iron and steel industry failed; and though the stimulus of war demands caused a rapid development of that industry after 1914, it is still unable to supply the country's needs. The war led also to some development of chemical industries, oil and water power. India has today over a million factory workers, and the Calcutta jute mills are large-scale units. But industrialism has touched scarcely more than the fringe of Indian life as yet; banking and finance are little developed, and the factory worker is often a villager who has come to town for a few weeks or months in order to earn money to supplement the inadequate income of the farm.

The same is true of China. Attempts at factory spinning of cotton were made as early as 1860 and were successful after 1880. These early mills were owned by Chinese masters, who gathered in their kinsfolk and thus retained something of the family unit. After China's defeat by Japan foreign capital was invested in cotton mills, and a large spinning industry – half Japanese, partly Chinese and slightly British – grew up in the Shanghai area. In that region about 250 factories now exist making textiles and a wide range of other consumer goods, including even fountain pens and gramophones; but elsewhere there has been little industrialization, except in Manchuria under Japanese influence.

The rapidity of the modernization of Japan seems to make the phrase industrial revolution particularly applicable in its case; but it is significant that the commercial and financial transformations have been more far-reaching than the strictly industrial. Even before 1868 important changes in economic organization had been taking place in Japan; throughout the eighteenth and the early nineteenth century the feudal system was gradually being transformed by the development of a money economy, including a wage system. Under the modern government of the Meiji era industrialization became one of the first objectives of economic policy. Government subsidies secured by borrowings abroad made possible the construction of railroads and later of public utilities, gas and electric power works. The government established model factories and schools for the training of workers. Nevertheless, the progress of industrialization was slow; not until after the Sino-Japanese and Russo-Japanese wars did Japan's factory industries develop on any large scale. The World War caused an enormous expansion of all industries and offered an opportunity for Japan to capture the markets of the Orient; but the troubled economic and political conditions of post-war years forced a considerable recession. In 1927 Japan had 49,000 factories employing 1,700,000 workers. The most important factory industries are silk reeling and cotton spinning; but the weaving of cotton is still preponderantly a domestic industry, while silk weaving is negligible. Raw silk remains Japan's principal export and the majority of the population is still agricultural or rural, engaging in handicraft industries as a subsidiary occupation. Japan is already experiencing difficulties in finding an outlet for its cotton yarns or textile goods in India or China, and the development of the heavy metallurgical industries is costly because of its lack of raw materials.

In one sense the vast changes in progress in Soviet Russia do not constitute an industrial revolution, since they do not represent the substitution of one form of industrial organization for another. But this industrialization of an agricultural country is in another sense completely revolutionary. It could occur of course only after the methods and instruments of industrialism had been fully worked out in other countries. The logic of large-scale production, the factory system, and the machine technique are being adopted more completely in Russia, through their extension to agriculture, than anywhere else. The pattern of industrialization, which has been much the same for most countries, is completely changed in Russia. The heavy industries are being developed first rather than last; industrialization, while depending on foreign aid and the exports necessary to pay for it, is not based on a foreign market for consumers' goods. The social consequences of the industrial revolution in Russia are also vastly different; great as the hardships involved may be they fall most heavily on such classes as the kulaks and the merchants, not on the factory worker. Russia possesses all the natural resources necessary for a most complete development of the machine industries; a labour force is in process of creation. It is easy to overestimate the rapidity of progress, but these changes do have a spectacular quality which the first industrial revolution never possessed even in retrospect.

In all lands where it came to displace an established industrial structure the industrial revolution ran a roughly similar course. The textile industry was usually the first to be affected, then the making of clothes, metal articles, and food-stuffs; the large-scale manufacture of iron and of steel represented often a distinct step forward but one not easy to take, while the manufacture of machines and producers' goods generally was a hazardous venture. Indeed it is this final step towards complete industrialization which has been most difficult for more recently industrialized countries. In lands coming late to industrialism the easiest success has been won in industries which process the natural or farm products, which produce simple wares such as blankets or plain cotton pieces or which enjoy the natural protection of distance from possible competitors.

Migration of industry from manual domestic or shop conditions to the factory varied in speed from industry to industry. Spinning went quickly; weaving, knitting, and some metal trades passed through a transitional workshop period, in which workers were gathered under one roof but continued to use the old equipment. In the clothing industries the sewing machine could be used in the home, and many women clung to the putting out system but had to submit to sweated conditions. The shoemaker and hand-loom weaver put up a long fight, and the victory of the laundry and bakery is still far from complete in Europe.

Dependence on coal and water power led to industrial concentration on the coalfields, river valleys, and such belts as the fall line in America. Water power had only a limited effect in causing concentration, for it strung the factories all along the banks of rapidly flowing rivers, and for certain textile-washing processes an ample supply of water was almost as important as a supply of fuel or power. Where water and coal were found together, as in the Pennine valleys and eastern Belgium, industry was spread over the whole region in villages or towns. For the metal industries location was determined by the coal supply, since it was easier to bring the metal to the coal than vice versa; but this involved the construction of adequate transport facilities, such as the railroad between Lorraine and the Ruhr.

The movement of population to the industrial areas still needs further study. But for England it is now evident that there was no simple mass transfer of people from the south and east to the north and west. The industrial towns grew by drawing workers in from the hinterland, and the void thus made was filled by people from slightly farther afield. Journeys were generally short, except in the case of the Irish who swarmed across the Irish Sea to Lancashire, Glasgow, and Yorkshire. Only later, when the railroads made longer journeys easier, was there any serious long-distance migration. In newer countries, such as the United States, native population was for long streaming away from the eastern industrial centres and a continual inflow of immigrants was necessary to insure an adequate labour supply.

Problems of urban health and housing were probably most acute in those towns which were the homes of the early spinning factories. In looking at them it should be remembered that until 1835 many British manufacturing centres had no adequate municipal government, that knowledge about the essentials of public health was scanty, that cheap production of pipes, bricks, and woodwork did not come until about 1840, that house building depended on the willingness of someone to sink capital in dwellings and that the rate of interest current or the profits to be made in industry might be more tempting than the return on house property. A glance at the housing of the poor in non-industrial towns of the eighteenth century and at the difficulties which have surrounded the provision of working-class dwellings since 1914 should provoke a more merciful judgement of the 'jerry builder' of the early nineteenth century. In the United States living conditions in the early textile towns of New England were very good; only with the coming of wave after wave of foreign labourers did the worst slum conditions appear.

Of labour conditions no easy generalization is possible. Long hours, child labour, employment of women, insanitary conditions, payment in truck, unemployment, low wages, capitalistic tyranny, labour unrest, industrial fatigue, occupational diseases, and the 'cash nexus' were not inventions of industrial factory capitalism. Night work was a new thing in the textile industries; but the only novelty about child labour was that children now worked in large groups, were subject to factory rather than parental discipline, discharged more responsible tasks, had to leave the hearth to work and were kept rigorously at their day or night tasks. It should be noted, however, that child labour was universally regarded as natural and that the children's earnings were larger in the factory than they had been at home. When child labour was forbidden, something else – education – had to be developed to fill the waking hours of the young. The hazards to life and limb might perhaps have been prevented before they were attacked by legislation but they had first to be recognized as such, and the apathy towards them was as marked among the operatives as among employers. Such conditions and attitudes repeated themselves in most countries or regions where the factory system was introduced.

As to wages and employment light and shade alternate. In the early stages the new industries, especially cotton and pottery, seem to have paid much higher wages than were prevalent in the older industries, and the demand for hand-loom weavers to cope with the flood of machine-made yarn raised the rates paid for weaving. In England the long war with France lifted many nominal wages and some real ones, but the slump after Waterloo lowered levels in industry and agriculture alike. The hand-loom weaver and some other manual workers suffered when they stuck to their benches in face of the machine; but elsewhere conditions seem to have improved because of rising wages and falling prices after about 1820 or 1830. Some occupations passed from male to female hands, but new occupations were opened up and old ones expanded – metallurgy, mechanical engineering, the construction and operation of railroads, shipbuilding, mining, building – and the opportunities for skilled, well-paid work multiplied accordingly.

In short, the industrial revolution increased rather than decreased the material welfare of the mass of the population; but some sections suffered from the transition, war, and business fluctuations disturbed wages and prices and the dangers latent in the employee's lot became apparent. Unfortunately much of our view of the social aspects of the revolution is drawn from reports of official investigations, which in their very nature are full of complaints and grievances. From them one can paint the industrial revolution as 'an orgy of soulless cupidity' (Tawney) and assume that to be the whole picture. But quantitative studies such as that by Clapham; detailed business studies of Oldknow, Owen, Wedgwood, Boulton, Gott, Krupp, and others; and a more detailed knowledge of pre-revolutionary conditions tone down the picture and make at least some of the industrial leaders appear more like human beings and less like incarnations of ruthless self-interest. Moreover, it is still far from certain how much the revolution was 'a triumph of the spirit of enterprise' (Tawney). Enterprise there was but not always triumph, and the industrial field was strewn with the wreckage of men who failed. The trouble with machinery that broke down, with workmen who refused to use it, with customers who demanded long credit yet refused to pay their debts, with booms that burst, with banks that refused any more loans, with wars that closed markets, all made the road stony. Inadequate supplies of working capital wrecked many a venture, and when a successful period came the profits had to be ploughed back into the business. The industrial revolution has not yet been studied through the records of bankruptcy, but enough is known to show on what a treacherous sea the entrepreneur of the early machine age launched his boat.

3 The Causes of the Industrial Revolution: An Essay in Methodology[1]

R. M. HARTWELL

[This article was first published in *The Economic History Review*, 2nd series, Vol. XVIII, No. 1 (1965).]

I

J. H. Clapham wrote in 1910 that, 'Even if . . . the history of "the" industrial revolution is a "thrice squeezed orange", there remains an astonishing amount of juice in it'.[2] Indeed, half a century later interest in the industrial revolution is increasing, not waning, and, as a topic for research it seems still to be strangely unworked. The gaps in the literature – for example, the history of any major industry for the years 1760–1860 – are more obvious than the achievements. The twentieth century has been remarkable for historical productivity, for the increasing quantity and range of source materials available, for the growing sophistication of techniques, and for the large-scale growth in numbers of *professional* economic historians, with their own societies, journals, university departments, and degrees, but there still is relative ignorance about many major problems of the industrial revolution, and in lieu of detailed investigation into their solutions, inevitably much speculation. It is, of course, easier to speculate than to do research, and although speculation is a good guide for research, too many insights established speculatively have tended to become dogma, and their acceptance as revealed truth has often inhibited that

[1] I am indebted to Professors E. F. Söderlund and L. E. Davis, and particularly to Dr A. R. Hall, for criticism and advice during the writing of this paper.
[2] J. H. Clapham 'The Transference of the Worsted Industry from Norfolk to the West Riding', *The Economic Journal*, xx (1910), p. 195.

E

very research which alone could establish their validity.[1] Nevertheless, historians of the industrial revolution have ranged widely, from inquiries into the first use of the term and the dating of the upswing, through local, business, and industrial histories, to inconclusive and often confused discussion about causes and consequences. The most lively literature has been concerned with the way of life and the standard of living during industrialization, i.e. with the consequences of the industrial revolution, and the important problem of determining why the revolution occurred at all, and why it occurred in England, i.e. with the causes of the industrial revolution, has not received its warranted attention. Indeed, on the origins of the industrial revolution, the historians have been neither very illuminating nor particularly argumentative, being seemingly happy to accept simultaneously a number of suggested solutions without testing their mutual consistency, either deductively or empirically. This is surprising. On any historical accounting, the industrial revolution is one of the great discontinuities of history; it would not be implausible indeed, to claim that it has been the greatest.[2] The transition, first in England and then throughout Europe and increasingly throughout the world, from stable subsistence or low *per capita* real incomes to sustained increases in *per capita* real incomes, and the revolution in industrial technology and organization, and the radical change in the structure of national economies, and the massive growth of population, represent a fundamental discontinuity in world economic

[1] Good examples of now questioned dogma are (*a*) the relationship between enclosure and labour supply, (*b*) the influence of medicine on the death rate, (*c*) the yeoman origins of entrepreneurs, (*d*) the unqualified assumption that there was a *laissez faire* policy during the industrial revolution. Untested dogma, still to be investigated thoroughly, include the following: (*a*) the assumed importance of international trade as providing the main or crucial increase in demand during the industrial revolution, (*b*) the assumption that there was a marked increase in *per capita* savings (investment) in the eighteenth century, (*c*) the assumption that there was a turning point, (*d*) the assumptions that in the eighteenth century social overheads were financed by market funds and industrial investment by profits. Further research may show that these latter assumptions are correct; at the moment to assert their truth is to be dogmatic.

[2] See Carlo Cipolla, *The Economic History of World Population* (Pelican Books, London, 1962), pp. 24–31, who also argues (p. 29) that the industrial revolution created a 'deep breach . . . in the continuity of the historical process'.

development. But perhaps failure to explain does not indicate lack of interest or effort? Perhaps the problem of *explaining* the origins of the industrial revolution in England is too complex for even the most talented historian to disentangle. Or, making the problem equally insoluble, perhaps the meagreness of data, particularly statistical data, makes causal analysis and the measurement of the relative importance of 'causes' impossible. Indeed, the understanding of economic growth has also been found impossible by the economists, who have been unable to formulate satisfactory theories of growth and to relate them to practical policies for growth. Alfred Marshall failed to produce his projected fourth volume, *Progress: its Economic Conditions*;[1] no economist since has been more successful. However, the historians at least have long had their eyes on what today is admitted by the economists to be a major problem; the economists, in contrast, ignored the problems of growth for more than a century. Only since 1945 have the economists again been interested in what was the major theme of Adam Smith's foundation text of the study of economics, first published in 1776: 'an inquiry into the nature and causes of the wealth of nations'.

The economists' renewed interest in history has been the result, partly of the Keynesian revolution (the logical outcome of which have been the growth models, attempts to define the relationship between inputs of capital, labour, and technical knowledge and rates of growth of output), and partly of the need to understand, for practical reasons, the problems of the underdeveloped economies of the world. The results for economic history have been important. History now seems useful to the economist because it provides (or should provide) a large source of information about past economic growth, bountiful facts for processing into practical generalizations for growth.[2]

[1] See Preface to *Money, Credit and Commerce* (London, 1923), p. vi, where Marshall stated his intention to complete his *Principles* with a further volume on 'the possibilities of social advance'.

[2] See, for example, the following books by economists on economic growth with historical sections: G. M. Meier and R. E. Baldwin, *Economic Development. Theory, History, Policy* (New York, 1957), Part 2; B. Higgins, *Economic Development. Problems, Principles and Policies* (London, 1959), Part 3; A. K. Cairncross, *Factors in Economic Development* (London, 1962), Parts II and III.

These empiricists of growth have revived, to some extent, an historical school in economics. At the same time they are beginning to stimulate a more theoretical school in economic history, especially in the United States of America. Economic history has always been concerned largely with the documentation, description, and explanation of what the economists call economic growth, and with so much empirical and theoretical literature on growth by the economists now available, some historians are turning towards the economists for guidance. The main result should be to make the historian aware of the unsystematic nature of many of his explanations of growth, of how often his inferences have been outrageous extrapolations from inadequate data, often, indeed, '*a priori* assumptions made specious by an unsystematic and unscientific marshalling of unreliable data'.[1]

Thus, for example, 'explanations' of the industrial revolution have consisted mainly of suggesting a large number of variables, sometimes relationships between variables, and usually of attributing the crucial discontinuity to the aggregate effects of the autonomous variation of *one* important variable. The most popular explanation has taken the form of a simple capital accumulation model. It is fair to say that the historians, in their detailed analyses, have suggested *many* 'causal factors', yet nearly all have sought 'a main cause' and have elevated *one* variable, explicitly or implicitly, to the role of *chief cause*. The student, faced with a shelf of authorities, each with a different cause, or a different combination of causes of the industrial revolution, may well be excused for this confusion. Recently, for example, a meeting of economic historians, arranged by *Past and Present*, to discuss the origins of the industrial revolution, agreed that they had no answer to that problem, and called for more research 'to clarify the problems of capital formation . . . and of effective demand'; on neither of these problems, nor on two others – the problems of 'social structure' and of 'why the revolution occurred first in Britain' – was there any general

---

[1] I am generalizing here a remark of H. T. Davis about Marx in his *The Analysis of Economic Time Series* (Bloomington, Indiana, 1941), p. 571.

agreement, or, if the printed account is an accurate guide, much useful discussion.[1]

II

The most important general accounts of the industrial revolution have been those of Toynbee,[2] Mantoux,[3] and Ashton,[4] with significant contributions also by Bowden,[5] Fay,[6] Beales,[7] and Heaton.[8] Beard's slender volume on the industrial revolution is worth mentioning only because it was written so early.[9] Since the time when economic history began to develop as a formal discipline in the last quarter of the nineteenth century, however, most of Britain's best-known economic historians have written, at one time or another, about the industrial revolution; for example, Cunningham, Ashley, Unwin, the Hammonds, Clapham, Clark, Redford, Lipson, Court, Chambers, and John.[10] Recent contributions have been made by Rostow,

[1] *Past and Present*, no. 17 (April 1960), pp. 71–81.

[2] A. Toynbee, *Lectures on the Industrial Revolution of the Eighteenth Century in England* (London, 1884).

[3] P. Mantoux, *The Industrial Revolution in the Eighteenth Century* (English translation of the French original of 1906, London, 1928).

[4] T. S. Ashton, *The Industrial Revolution, 1760–1830* (Home University Library, Oxford, 1948).

[5] W. Bowden, *Industrial Society in England towards the End of the Eighteenth Century* (New York, 1925).

[6] C. R. Fay, *Great Britain from Adam Smith to the Present Day* (London, 1928).

[7] H. L. Beales, *The Industrial Revolution, 1750–1850* (London, 1928).

[8] H. Heaton, 'Industrial Revolution', *Encyclopaedia of the Social Sciences* (New York, 1948), Vol. 8, pp. 3–13.

[9] C. Beard, *The Industrial Revolution* (London, 1901).

[10] W. Cunningham, *The Growth of English Industry and Commerce in Modern Times*, Vol. III, *Laissez Faire* (Cambridge, 1882); W. J. Ashley, *The Economic Organization of England* (London, 1914), Chapter VII; G. Unwin, *Samuel Oldknow and the Arkwrights. The Industrial Revolution at Stockport and Marples* (Manchester, 1924): J. L. and B. Hammond, *The Rise of Modern Industry* (London, 1925), Part II; J. H. Clapham, 'The Industrial Revolution and the Colonies', *Cambridge History of the British Empire*, Vol. II (Cambridge, 1940); G. N. Clark, *The Idea of the Industrial Revolution* (Glasgow, 1953); A. Redford, *The Economic History of England, 1760–1860* (London, 1931); E. Lipson, *The Growth of English Society* (London, 1949); W. H. B. Court, *Concise Economic History of Britain* (Cambridge, 1954); J. D. Chambers, *The Workshop of the World* (Home University Library, Oxford, 1961); and A. H. John, *The Industrial Development of South Wales, 1750–1850* (Cardiff, 1950).

Deane and Cole, and Habakkuk and Deane.[1] All these, and many others too numerous to mention, have attempted to give some explanation of the conditions which first gave rise to English industrialization. While most of these historians have stressed technological change, and nearly all have given primary importance to capital accumulation, some also have stressed *laissez-faire*, and most have said something about the importance of market expansion (usually abroad). In addition to economic variables, however, the industrial revolution has been attributed to the protestant ethic, to the commercial bias of English science and law and to the flexibility of the English social structure. To some, English leadership was no more than an accident of geography, the combination of a fortunate site for trading and favourable factor endowments. The following table lists the factors which the historians have used to explain the acceleration of growth in the eighteenth century.

Table: *Forces Making for Growth*

1. *Capital Accumulation:* increased savings (from commerce and agriculture), low interest rates, increased investment (e.g. in transport); ploughing-back of high proportion of increased industrial profits; increased investment from profit inflation; better mobilizing of savings because of improved financial institutions; economy of savings (e.g. inventories) because of improved transport.

2. *Innovations – Changes in the Technology and Organization of Agriculture and Industry:* new and improved machinery; new sources of power; more roundabout and larger-scale production (e.g. enclosures and factories) with greater division of labour; industrial localization (external economies).

3. *Fortunate Factor Endowments:* coal, iron ore, and other minerals necessary for industrialization; favourable size of the economy (short hauls); favourable trading site for growth mar-

[1] W. W. Rostow, *The Process of Economic Growth* (Oxford, 1960, enlarged edition of 1953 original); P. Deane and W. A. Cole, *British Economic Growth, 1688–1959. Trends and Structure* (Cambridge, 1962); and H. J. Habakkuk and P. Deane, 'The Take-off in Britain', *The Economics of Take-Off into Sustained Growth*, W. W. Rostow (ed.) (London, 1963).

kets (America and Asia); skilled labour force; increasing labour inputs (because of absolute increase in population, and a relatively larger industrial labour force, the result of greater agricultural productivity); entrepreneurial and inventing talent in good supply.

4. *Laissez-faire*: long-term changes in philosophy, religion, science, and law, culminating in the eighteenth century in secularism, rationalism, and economic individualism; propagandists for free enterprise and receptive statesmen; Adam Smith; social mobility.

5. *Market Expansion*: increasing foreign trade; increasing domestic consumption because of (*a*) increasing population and (*b*) rising real incomes; urbanization; improved transport which (*a*) lowered costs and prices, stimulating demand and (*b*) unified and increased the market; relatively lower prices of industrial goods, increasing demand.

6. *Miscellaneous*: Continental wars which favoured English and discouraged continental development; 'the bounty of God' (the decline of plague and the good harvests of the 1730s and 1740s); the autonomous growth of knowledge; 'the English genius'.

Not all historians have listed all these 'forces making for growth'; and, moreover, however long the list of any particular historian, there has been an almost irresistible urge for that same historian to stress *one* force above all others, and to assume, at least implicitly, that growth was the result of variations in that factor operating in an aggregate fashion on the whole economy to produce a clearly recognizable discontinuity in English economic history; in other words, to produce both a turning-point and also a take-off.

Modern discussion of the causes of the industrial revolution dates from 1884 when Arnold Toynbee's lectures were published. Toynbee had a turning-point – 'Previously to 1760 the old industrial system obtained in England' – and a simple explanation – 'The essence of the Industrial Revolution is the substitution of competition for the medieval regulations which had previously controlled the production and distribution of wealth' – but he gave no clear chronology or analysis of the events leading up to 1760. To Toynbee the change in economic policy, from mercantilism to *laissez-faire*, was the cause of industrialization, and Adam Smith was largely responsible. '*The Wealth of Nations* and the steam engine destroyed the old world and built a new one', he wrote, underlining the importance of technical change while making it quite clear that freedom of enterprise was the prime mover. 'Without competition, no progress could be possible,' he argued.[1] Writing at the same time as Toynbee, W. Cunningham in his *The Growth of English Industry and Commerce in Modern Times* also labelled the section of his history on the eighteenth and nineteenth centuries 'Laissez Faire', and began it with an account of the industrial revolution. After noting the magnitude of the social and economic changes that followed from industrialization, Cunningham generalized: 'The introduction of expensive implements, or processes, involves a large outlay; it is not worth while for any man, however energetic, to make an attempt, unless he has a considerable command of capital, and has access to large markets. In the eighteenth century these conditions were being more and more realized'.[2] To Cunningham, then, the conjuncture of increasing capital accumulation and expanding markets were the strategic factors in England's economic advance. Another pioneer economic historian W. J. Ashley, in his *The Economic Organization of England*, included a chapter on 'The Industrial Revolution and Freedom of Contract', and dated change from the agricultural revolution which led to 'a vast increase in the production of food, and this increase rendered possible the expansion of our population, which was stimulated by the growth of factory industries, offering employment to children.'[3] To Ashley the increasing productivity of agriculture was both the prerequisite and the promoter of industrialization.

The most detailed study of the industrial revolution remains today that of Paul Mantoux, published in 1906. To Mantoux, the industrial revolution was 'essentially a commercial pheno-

---

[1] Toynbee, op. cit., pp. 64, 204–5.   [2] Cunningham, op. cit., p. 610.
[3] Ashley, op. cit., p. 136.

menon, and was connected with the gradual hold obtained by merchants over industry. Not only was it accompanied, but it was prepared, by the expansion of trade and credit.' The advent of machinery was 'an inevitable result of the extension of trade'. But Mantoux also stressed the importance of agriculture, classing agricultural improvement with commercial expansion as necessary 'preparatory changes'. 'The growth of great industrial centres would have been impossible if agricultural production had not been so organized as to provide for the needs of a large industrial population.' To Mantoux the industrial revolution was caused by the expansion of trade and credit reacting on the organization and technology of industry. 'Division of labour,' he wrote, 'varies with the size of the market.'[1] That market expansion forced development was also the view of A. Redford, who wrote that 'the fundamental stimulus to industrial change and technological innovation in England during the seventeenth and eighteenth centuries arose almost certainly from the effects of that progressive widening of the world's markets which followed the geographical discoveries . . . acting upon the highly specialized economy of a country rich in coal and metallic ores, and endowed with an enterprising and adaptable people'.[2]

Similar views, but more explicitly stressing the expansion of *demand*, were expressed by W. Bowden and E. W. Gilboy. Witt Bowden argued that increasing wealth at home and abroad had increased demand beyond the limits which the traditional forms of industry could supply. 'It was in respect to the demand for English goods,' he wrote, 'that the eighteenth century differed most radically from earlier periods. Pressure for goods was felt alike by the manufacturer, the trader and the farmer.' 'So large was the demand at home, and so extensive were the overseas markets controlled by Englishmen, that without new methods of production, "no exertions of the manufacturers could have answered the demands of trade".'[3] E. W. Gilboy saw the main stimulus in increasing home demand: 'Changing consumption standards, the increase of population and shifting of individuals

<hr>

[1] Mantoux, op. cit., pp. 487, 137, 190.
[2] Redford, op. cit., p. 3. [3] Bowden, op. cit., p. 65.

from class to class, and a rise in real income provided a stimulus to the expansion of industry which must not be underestimated.'[1]

More eclectic explanations of the origins of the industrial revolution have been given by E. Lipson and T. S. Ashton. Lipson accepted that 'the explanation is commonly found in the expansion of . . . overseas trade with a far-flung commercial empire in America, India, and Africa, which together with the Continent of Europe supplied markets for . . . manufactures', and added five other factors: capital accumulation, entrepreneurial ability, population growth, the early exploitation of coal, and a home market 'where property was widely diffused and whose standard of comfort was substantial without being luxurious'.[2] Ashton's introduction to his *The Industrial Revolution* summarized the great changes that occurred in England after 1760, and sought their origins in a fortunate combination of favourable factors. 'The conjuncture of growing supplies of land, labour, and capital made possible the expansion of industry; coal and steam provided the fuel and power for large-scale manufacture; low rates of interest, rising prices, and high expectations of profit offered the incentive. But behind and beyond these material and economic factors lay something more. Trade with foreign parts had widened men's views of the world, and science their conception of the universe: the industrial revolution was also a revolution in ideas.' In particular, *The Wealth of Nations* inspired new attitudes: 'It was under its influence that the idea of a more or less fixed volume of trade and employment, directed and regulated by the State, gave way – gradually and with many setbacks – to thoughts of unlimited progress in a free and expanding economy.' But Ashton too sought a main cause, reckoning that, 'If we seek – it would be wrong to do so – for a single reason why the pace of economic development quickened about the middle of the

---

[1] E. W. Gilboy, 'Demand as a Factor in the Industrial Revolution', *Facts and Factors in Economic History* (Harvard University Press, 1932), p. 639. This is an important and neglected essay, partly, no doubt, because of the rarity of the volume in which it is published.

[2] Lipson, op. cit., p. 189 *et seq.*

eighteenth century, it is to this [the lower rate at which capital could be obtained] we must look.'[1]

This list by no means exhausts the historical writing about the origins of the industrial revolution; it is meant to be representative rather than comprehensive. Some recent contributions are now added, to demonstrate that the method in this historical inquiry has not changed, particularly the *penchant* for a simple explanation. H. J. Habakkuk and P. Deane, for example, after considering and rejecting the possibility of population growth, technical improvements or increasing investment effecting the breakthrough, come down in favour of international trade.[2] P. Deane and W. A. Cole, however, reject increasing international trade as the promoter of growth, and find rather that agricultural change and population growth play the vital roles in the 'mechanics of eighteenth-century growth'.[3] A. H. John finds the key to change in agriculture,[4] while J. D. Chambers sees industrialization as the response to an autonomous increase in population.[5] Finally, there is W. W. Rostow, to whom the industrial revolution was the result of a rise in the rate of productive investment, and the development of a narrow range of substantial manufacturing sectors operating in favourable institutional environment which quickly transmitted change throughout the economy.[6]

The mainspring of the industrial revolution may lie deep in the long history of European civilization, the only civilization (Japan excepted) yet to achieve industrialization, but a shorter-term process of economic change in eighteenth-century England also has to be analysed. In the historians' accounts of the industrial revolution there has been little attempt to determine the strategic variables of the economy of England and their

[1] Ashton, op. cit., pp. 21, 22, 11.
[2] Habakkuk and Deane, op. cit., pp. 77–80.
[3] Deane and Cole, op. cit., pp. 82–97.
[4] A. H. John, 'Aspects of English Economic Growth in the First Half of the Eighteenth Century', *Essays in Economic History*, Vol. II, E. M. Carus-Wilson (ed.) (London, 1962), p. 373.
[5] J. D. Chambers, 'Population Change in a Provincial Town: Nottingham 1700–1800', *Studies in the Industrial Revolution*, L. S. Pressnell (ed.) (London, 1960), p. 101.
[6] Rostow, op. cit., Chapters 11 and 12.

functional relationships, less attempt to distinguish and weight exogenous and endogenous factors causing change, and no attempt to construct a dynamic model of the economy which could explain the process of growth. A satisfactory account of the industrial revolution would describe the economy before industrialization, analyse its structural relationships, and identify its external constraints. The rate of growth of output, in a mechanical sense, was determined by the rate of growth of population, by the rate of capital accumulation, and by changes in the technology and organization of agriculture and industry. However, there are no accurate and few plausible estimates of these variables: some attempts to determine population growth,[1] one attempt to estimate capital growth,[2] and no serious attempt at all to measure technical change.[3] A major problem is to determine to what extent growth was the result of endogenous or exogenous forces; to what extent, for example, independent variables like an autonomous growth of foreign trade or an increase in population growth for non-economic reasons promoted economic growth is not known. Certainly a force, or forces for change – whether internal and/or external – were sufficiently great over the course of half a century to alter the structure of the economy and to increase and sustain the rate of growth. The historians have identified an impressive range of forces making for growth, but they have been unable to reach any agreement on the relative importance of those forces, or how they operated in a process of economic change. In particular, they have not demonstrated how their favoured endogenous one variable model of eighteenth-century growth could have worked. Indeed, the historians have no agreed definition of the industrial revolution (in terms of rate of growth of output, or changing economic structure, or technical change, etc.), have not explained the turning-point,[4]

---

[1] G. S. L. Tucker, 'English Pre-Industrial Population Trends', *The Economic History Review*, 2nd series, XVI, no. 2 (December 1963).

[2] Deane and Cole, op. cit., Chapter VIII.

[3] But see S. Lilley, *Men, Machines and History* (London, 1948), pp. 207–26, for a rare attempt to measure 'the relative invention rate'.

[4] J. U. Nef, *War and Human Progress* (London, 1950) discusses the turning-point in Chapter 15.

and have not analysed 'the mechanics of eighteenth century growth'.

III

Economists also may not have succeeded in their analyses of economic growth, but at least their efforts have been systematic; they have attempted to relate functionally the appropriate variables of growth, and although there is still no set of principles that can be labelled 'the theory of economic growth', there are rigorous if simple models of growth which are continually being made more complicated (i.e. more realistic). The economists also have collected an enormous amount of statistical data, particularly time-series, to illustrate the long-term behaviour of economies and whose systematic analysis has provided insights and generalizations about historic growth.[1] Can the economists, therefore, help the historians? After all, the factors which interest the economist are just those which have featured prominently in the writings of the historian; particularly the increasing accumulation of capital, the progress of technology, the change in social environment, and the growth of demand (for example, through population growth). Can a wedding of economic and historical thinking on the roles of these variables help to explain the origins of the industrial revolution?

1. *Capital Accumulation*

To Adam Smith the fundamental determinant of growth was the rate of capital formation, and this rate was proportional to the rate of investment. 'The annual produce of the land and labour of any nation,' he wrote, 'can be increased in its value by no other means, but by increasing either the numbers of its productive labourers, or the productive powers of those labourers who had before been employed. The number of its productive labourers, it is evident, can never be much increased, but in consequence of an increase of capital, or of the funds

---

[1] To this work, for example, S. Kuznets has devoted his academic life.

destined for maintaining them. The productive powers of the same number of labourers cannot be increased, but in consequence either of some addition and improvement to those machines and instruments which facilitate and abridge labour; or of a more proper division and distribution of employment. In either case an additional capital is almost always required.'[1] The importance of capital formation for growth has been largely accepted by all economists and historians[2] since Adam Smith, and it has been argued recently that the industrial revolution was no more than an acceleration in the rate of capital formation. A. Lewis has written, for example, that, 'All countries which are now relatively developed have at some time in the past gone through a period of rapid acceleration, in the course of which the rate of annual net investment has moved from 5 per cent or less to 12 per cent or more. This is what we mean by an Industrial Revolution.'[3] But the idea (even if true) of growth as a result of the savings rate and the aggregate capital–output ratio conceals more problems than it solves for a rapidly changing economy.[4] Moreover, there is scepticism that capital accumulation *per se* will necessarily produce growth; indeed the fundamental question – the extent to which capital is indispensable for growth – has not yet been answered, and certainly post-war experience in underdeveloped countries has provided no answer. The relationship between investment and the growth of output is not uniform; there have been wide varieties of experience, both between nations, and also in the same nation over time.[5] And even when growth has followed capital accumulation, the important problem remains of determining how complementary inputs (for example, labour and raw material supplies) adjusted smoothly to the requirements of

[1] A. Smith, *The Wealth of Nations* (Cannan Edition, London, 1904), Vol. I, p. 325.

[2] W. Cunningham, for example, was 'inclined to think that this [capital formation] may be advantageously treated as the dominating factor in Economic History'.

[3] A. Lewis, *The Theory of Economic Growth* (London, 1955), p. 208.

[4] See, for example, the article of A. Fishlow, 'Empty Economic Stages', *The Economic Journal*, LXXV (March 1965).

[5] See, for example, A. Maddison, *Economic Growth in the West* (London, 1964), Chapter III.

growth. However, perhaps the most damaging argument against this conception of growth concerns the propensity to save. Rather than increased savings and investment causing growth, both are more likely to be the result of growth. In eighteenth-century England, for example, a main source of capital for industry was reinvested profit; other sources were banks and merchants, who grew with industry;[1] in other words, the rate of investment was dependent on the rate of growth, the ability to save was not autonomous and accompanied rather than preceded growth. The amount of capital needed is debated; S. Pollard claims, for example, that a substantial diversion of resources was necessary for capital formation,[2] while M. Postan that 'by the beginning of the eighteenth century there were enough rich people in the country to finance an economic effort far in excess of the modest activities of the leaders of the Industrial Revolution'.[3] Unfortunately reliable evidence about the rate of aggregate capital accumulation in the eighteenth century is meagre, although Deane and Cole have tried to demonstrate that the rate of *per capita* capital accumulation in England did not increase markedly.[4] The fact that *after* 1780 the economy could finance both increasing industrialization and a large war expenditure, without serious inflation, confirms this view that the capital needs of early industrialization were modest.[5] Thus there seems to be little theoretical or historical justification for assuming that the industrial revolution in England was the result of a notable acceleration in capital accumulation.

One theory which should be mentioned, if only because it had the backing of J. M. Keynes, argues that the steady price rise between 1750 and 1790 inflated profits, increased savings

---

[1] See H. Heaton, 'Financing the Industrial Revolution', *Bulletin of the Business Historical Society*, XI (February 1937) and S. Pollard, 'Fixed Capital in the Industrial Revolution', *The Journal of Economic History*, XXXIV (September 1964).

[2] Ibid., pp. 299, 314; also, 'Investment, Consumption and the Industrial Revolution', *The Economic History Review*, 2nd series, XI, no. 2 (December 1958), pp. 215–16.

[3] M. Postan, 'Recent Trends in the Accumulation of Capital', *The Economic History Review*, 1st series, VI, No. 1 (October 1935), p. 2.

[4] Deane and Cole, op. cit., p. 304.

[5] I am indebted to Professor G. S. L. Tucker for this point.

and accelerated capital formation. Keynes wrote in *The Treatise on Money* that, 'It is the teaching of this Treatise that the wealth of nations is enriched not during Income inflations, but during Profit inflations – at times, that is to say, when prices are running away from costs'. E. J. Hamilton has provided historical backing for this thesis and has argued that the profit inflation after 1750 caused the industrial revolution. But disaggregating the price rise shows that money wages rose more than industrial prices and less than agricultural prices; if anything, there was pressure on industrial profits in the second half of the eighteenth century. More generally, two economists have argued, on theoretical and historical grounds, that nowhere in history is there evidence of a clear wage-lag that cannot be explained by real or monetary factors.[1]

2. *Technical Change*

i. INVENTION. Many economists now believe that the rate of growth is a function of the rate of technical change and its application to industry.[2] Historically, however, it is difficult to separate technological progress and capital accumulation. Most new technology during the industrial revolution, for example, was embodied in new or improved capital goods; thus, there was a close relationship between investment, capital formation, technical progress, and increases in output. However, if there was no great increase in *per capita* accumulation, the increase in *per capita* output must have come from the use of more productive or better-organized equipment. But the use of better equipment presupposes invention and innovation, and the problems remain of determining why appropriate inventions were made when they were made, how knowledge of them spread,[3] and

---

[1] J. M. Keynes, *A Treatise on Money* (London, 1930), Vol. II, Chapter 30, and E. J. Hamilton, 'Profit Inflation and the Industrial Revolution', *Quarterly Journal of Economics*, LVI (1941–42), pp. 257 *et seq.*, for the profit-inflation theory; R. A. Kessel and A. A. Alchian, 'The Meaning and Validity of the Inflation-Induced Lag of Wages', *American Economic Review*, L, No. 1 (March 1960) for criticism.

[2] For example, R. Solow, S. Fabricant and A. Abramovitz appear to do so.

[3] Very little systematic historical work has been done on technical diffusion; for example, at the general level of eighteenth-century technical sophistication, how much technical change was *independent technical evolution* rather than *diffusion* is not known.

why and how entrepreneurs were able to embody those inventions in profitable enterprises when they did. The process of invention, however, has defied systematic analysis. T. S. Ashton has pointed out that although 'invention appears at every stage of human history . . . it rarely thrives in a community of simple peasants or unskilled manual labourers'.[1] Eighteenth-century England had a relatively advanced society and economy and it is not surprising that invention could flourish there. However, what of its timing and direction? Certainly the *kind* of invention and the *frequency* of invention are conditioned by the environment, by the social context with its incentives and opportunities, by the state of growth of knowledge, by 'the interaction of fundamental ideas and technical possibilities',[2] and by the stimulus of practical problems. But such general acknowledgements, and a study of the inventions of the eighteenth-century, do not reveal the sources of invention, nor, in many cases, reasons for the directions which invention took.[3] Nevertheless the connexion between technical change and output in the eighteenth century can be discerned. A listing of the important technical advances of the century shows two things: (1) the advances are made on a broad front – in textiles, basic metallurgy, mining, transport, agriculture, and power production – suggesting that the revolution in technology was not the product of any single intellectual or industrial stimulus, but rather the result of a growing awareness of the potentialities generally of technical progress; (2) there were two important clusters of inventions, one early, one late in the century. The coke-smelting of iron, the Newcomen engine and Kay's flying shuttle all came before 1733. The great concentration, however, is after 1768: the Jenny (1768), the Water Frame (1769), the boring

[1] Ashton, op. cit., p. 15.
[2] A. C. Crombie (ed.), *Scientific Change* (London, 1963), p. 4.
[3] The classical theory of the direction of invention argues that inventive effort is distributed according to relative factor prices, i.e. is either capital, labour, or raw-material saving in bias according to relative prices and price changes. And although Ashton (for the eighteenth century) and Habakkuk (for the nineteenth) have tried to demonstrate this thesis, the attempts are not convincing. A chronological chart of inventions over these two centuries shows no pattern at all, let alone a systematic relation to factor prices. Ashton, op. cit., p. 91; H. J. Habakkuk, *American and British Technology in the 19th Century* (Cambridge, 1962).

F

mill (1775), the improved steam engine (1776–1781), the mule (1779), the seed drill (1782), cotton printing machinery (1783), iron puddling (1784), the first useful threshing machine (1786), and the improved lathe (1794). Most of these inventions took time to spread, but in this period the time-lag between invention and innovation shortened, the 'rate of improvement' in technology increased,[1] the combined effect of so many inventions over such a wide field was cumulatively impressive, and the rapid application of three important inventions – iron puddling, cotton spinning, and the steam engine – had immediate quantitative effects on the output of key sectors of the economy after 1780. The upturn in industrial production in the last quarter of the century followed these important technical changes.[2]

ii. INNOVATION. If invention as a social process is difficult to analyse, innovation is narrowly economic in motivation. Innovation depends on favourable economic conditions; on the supply side, on the availability of appropriate factor supplies and their prices, and on the demand side, on the existence of appropriate markets.[3] Obviously the availability of factors depends both on the physical and human resources of an economy, and also on the flexibility of the factor market. In significant senses England had a freer society and a freer economy in the eighteenth century than other European economies; there was greater security for property and enterprise; there was greater social mobility; the prevalent social attitudes (religious, political and economic) were relatively more favourable towards change; there was an increasing breakdown of medieval and mercantilist restrictions on trade and industry; improved communications made transport of men and materials easier; Great

[1] W. E. Salter, *Productivity and Technical Change* (Cambridge, 1960), p. 6, used the term 'rate of improvement' to indicate 'a given change in technical knowledge'.

[2] See T. S. Ashton, *An Economic History of England. The Eighteenth Century* (London, 1955), p. 125.

[3] J. A. Schumpeter has argued that growth is determined by the rate of innovation, a function of entrepreneurial activity, and that innovations appear discontinuously in groups or swarms; such a swarm began the industrial revolution. *The Theory of Economic Development* (Harvard, 1951), p. 223.

Britain constituted the largest free trade area in Europe. A freer economy meant the more effective working of the price mechanism; prices became more flexible and price changes became more efficient in promoting capital and labour mobility. In such circumstances profit became a more certain measure of economic efficiency, and enterprise was rewarded, making relative price changes effective in quickly encouraging or discouraging production. Here again, insight came originally from Adam Smith, who argued that if capital formation caused progress, the rate of capital formation depended on a favourable institutional environment, especially on free trade and competition. Free trade widened the market, permitted international division of labour, and increased productivity. Monopoly, on the other hand, was 'a great enemy to good management'.[1] It would be difficult, however, to measure the rate of growth of 'free enterprise' in the eighteenth century, although conceptually it could be measured, for example, by estimating the increasing proportion of total production which passed through the market. The untidy conclusion is that the English environment increasingly favoured enterprise and was increasingly effective in rewarding and punishing it. Thus in so far as historians have interpreted the differing histories of national economies in terms of the supply and characteristics of their entrepreneurs,[2] as the history of the industrial revolution in England has been interpreted, it can be argued rather that growth was not created by but allowed, enterprise to flourish.[3]

3. Social Change

Crucial change in the eighteenth century was dependent, not only on more productive equipment, not only on more

---

[1] Adam Smith, op. cit., I, p. 148.

[2] D. Landes, for example, attributes France's relative economic retardation in the nineteenth century to entrepreneurial shortcomings; 'French Entrepreneurship and Industrial Growth in the Nineteenth Century', *The Journal of Economic History*, IX, No. 1 (May 1949).

[3] As does Charles Wilson, 'The Entrepreneur in the Industrial Revolution in Britain', *History*, XLII (June 1957). It is remarkable *about Europe* that industrialization there was seldom hindered by lack of entrepreneurs or capital.

entrepreneurs, but also on changing values in society; in particular it was necessary to cross 'a threshold level of acceptance of novel methods'.[1] The changing values were reflected in changed social action that was economically significant: for example, at the top of the income structure more capital went into factories and less into country houses, while at the bottom more into new consumer goods and less in idleness, gin and a customary subsistence living standard. These switches in demand were the result partly of a rational economic reaction to price-changes, but partly also of a radical revision of those traditional attitudes which discouraged the fuller use of human and material resources. Men's minds turned *generally* from traditionalism to risk-taking and profit-making, from the acceptance of a customary way of life to striving for extra income and extra consumption; and although these changes were not independent of the economic opportunities offering, the emergence of 'pushing' entrepreneurs with 'disruptive innovating energy'[2] was the result of social forces, of changes in English society which rationalized and secularized human attitudes to the point that the pursuit of wealth dominated the minds of a much larger segment of English society than before, and the acceptance (if not the welcoming) of change was general. Some of the characteristics of this society have been described in the previous section, but the analysis of eighteenth-century social change and its relationship to eighteenth-century economic growth depends not only on detailed research by the historians, not yet done, but also on the theoretical guidance of economists and sociologists. However, although economists recognize that the requirements for economic growth involve both economic and social (or cultural) change, they have been quite unable to incorporate social forces into their systematic theories of development.[3] Sociologists, similarly, although they have posited certain general conditions which encourage social change (for example, the alleged importance for change

[1] Fishlow, op. cit., p. 123.

[2] The words are those of A. H. Cole.

[3] However, see E. E. Hagen, *On the Theory of Social Change; How Economic Growth begins* (Homewood, Illinois, 1962) for an attempt.

in society of social conflict), and although they have devoted much effort to study changes in social structure induced by industrialization, have raised more problems than they have solved; indeed, they look to history rather than to their own discipline for insight into the origins, the conditions, the rate, and the consequences of social change. There is no help for the historian of the industrial revolution in sociology.[1] There is no doubt, however, as H. L. Beales has insisted, that 'the analysis of the industrial revolution is still made too much in economic terms'.[2] But until there is considerably more research into the social factors which influenced economic change in eighteenth-century England, the historian of the industrial revolution must be content to assume their importance and to disguise his ignorance with a series of now well-known generalizations about religion and secularism,[3] science and rationalism, law and social mobility, government and freedom, and the consequential economically beneficial changes in social structure and action.

4. *Growth of Demand*

Adam Smith argued that the division of labour is limited by the extent of the market. 'As it is the power of exchanging that gives occasion to the division of labour; so the extent of this division must always be limited by the extent of that power, or, in other words, by the extent of the market.'[4] The importance of a high level and expansion of demand for growth was firmly postulated by Adam Smith, but over the long period of the classical dominance of economic theory, the importance of demand for growth was explained away by Say's law of markets, which postulated that production increased not only the supply

[1] See T. Bottomore, *Sociology. A Guide to Problems and Literature* (London, 1962), Chapter 17, for a discussion of the sociological literature on 'factors in social change'.

[2] Beales, op. cit., Introduction to 1958 edition, p. 20.

[3] See, for example, the critical examination of the alleged influence of Protestantism on economic life in K. Samuelsson, *Religion and Economic Life* (English translation, Stockholm, 1961).

[4] Adam Smith, op. cit., I, p. 19.

of goods in the market but also the demand for them.[1] Only with J. M. Keynes in the 1930s was the thesis advanced and universally accepted by the economists that incomes and employment are largely dependent on investment, that consumer spending has direct effects on profits and the incentive to invest. Even before Keynes some historians, perhaps still students of Adam Smith, realized, in the words of the Hammonds, that 'mass production demands popular consumption', and that 'the command of a wide market is essential to the organization of large-scale industry'.[2] But most historians of the industrial revolution, although implicitly recognizing the need to explain the disposal of an increasing output of consumer goods, have attributed greater importance to an increase in overseas trade than to an increase in home demand. The emphasis on international trade is understandable; there was a rapid expansion of exports in the third quarter of the eighteenth century,[3] and after a deceleration in the seventies a remarkable acceleration between 1780 and 1800; manufactures constituted a major part of exports, and a significant proportion of industrial output was exported; and the industries mainly dependent on the home economy expanded less rapidly than the major export industries.[4] However, much of the increased trade came from North America and the West Indies, colonies whose demand for English goods was largely derived from the English demand for colonial goods. Even so colonial trade was important because it increased the total size of the market available to English producers. It is not inappropriate, indeed, to speak of an Atlantic economy of the eighteenth century, with an aggregate market that permitted comparative advantage specialization in England which otherwise might not have been possible. The great foreign potential, nevertheless, was in Europe, with its 200 millions and 'towards the end of the century, England's cotton

---

[1] J. A. Schumpeter, *History of Economic Analysis* (London, 1954), p. 615 *et seq.* for a discussion of 'Say's Law of Markets'.

[2] J. L. and B. Hammond, op. cit., p. 67.

[3] R. Davis, 'English Foreign Trade, 1700–1774', *The Economic History Review*, 2nd series, xv, No. 2 (December 1962), p. 295.

[4] Deane and Cole, op. cit., pp. 41–50; also E. B. Schumpeter, *English Overseas Trade Statistics 1697–1808* (Oxford, 1960), p. 12.

and metal industries . . . were poised ready to invade not only the European but all other markets with their irresistible bundles of products of the Industrial Revolution'.[1]

However, foreign trade could only have accounted for a small though significant proportion of total industrial production in the years leading up to the industrial revolution. The largest growth market must have been the home market, especially since in the eighteenth century market expansion usually preceded industrial expansion. As Mantoux wrote, 'In those days progress in industry was almost impossible unless it was preceded by some commercial development.'[2] It was the relentless growth of domestic demand which stimulated industrial growth over a wide field, demand which was local and obvious and which had immediate response from industrial producers. The steadily expanding level of aggregate domestic demand was more important for growth than the more erratic growth of foreign trade in the years before 1780. Evidence for rising real wages in the first half of the century has been reviewed by various writers,[3] and was noted by Adam Smith in 1776: 'In Great Britain the real recompense of labour . . . the real quantities of the necessaries and conveniences of life which are given to the labourer, has increased considerably during the course of the present century.'[4] This increase in real wages owed much to agricultural improvements which date back well into the seventeenth century, and to a series of good harvests after 1730, both of which increased the disposable money income of the mass of Englishmen at a critical stage of development.[5]

[1] Davis, op. cit., p. 298.

[2] Mantoux, op. cit., p. 93.

[3] See, in particular, E. W. Gilboy, *Wages in Eighteenth Century England* (Harvard, 1934), and A. H. John, 'Aspects of English Economic Growth in the First Half of the Eighteenth Century', op. cit., p. 365.

[4] Adam Smith, op. cit., 1, p. 200.

[5] The questions of whether *an agricultural revolution* is a necessary prerequisite of *an industrial revolution*, and whether agriculture can be *a driving force* in *economic growth*, are still debated by the economists. Economic history shows that in Europe industrialization was preceded usually by a rise in agricultural productivity, but that the growth of the agricultural and non-agricultural sectors were intimately linked in a process of general economic growth (for example, through

A more productive agriculture not only increased real incomes and released resources to industry, it allowed more people to survive and the population of England to grow. What role did increasing population play in the industrial revolution? Historically population increase and economic growth go together, but although economic growth has always been accompanied by population growth, population growth has not always been accompanied by economic growth. Not only did the histories of England and Ireland between 1750 and 1850 demonstrate this, but in the hundred years since 1850, also, variations in the rate of growth of output in the countries of Europe have *not* shown any close relationship with population movements.[1] Historians, economists, and demographers are all interested in the relationship between industrialization and demographic change, for example during the industrial revolution, but this interest is frustrated by the absence of firm data on the population growth of the eighteenth century. It was almost certainly more food, the result of widespread agricultural improvements, which was responsible for the growth of population generally in Europe.[2] The combination in eighteenth-century England of improved agriculture *and* industrialization was unique; so too was the rate of increase of English population. It would seem, therefore, that population growth was the response to economic growth, and not an independent variable. In so far as the figures allow a regional breakdown, they confirm this view: the counties which were quickening industrially before the industrial revolution and which later became the main centres of industrial change, were already increasing their population faster than the rest of the country in the first half of the century; with industrialization these differentials increased.[3]

---

the industrial demand for agricultural raw materials). The economists' treatment of the problem is reviewed in C. Eicher and L. Witt (Editors), *Agriculture in Economic Development* (New York, 1964), especially Part I.

[1] Maddison, op. cit., p. 29 *et seq.*

[2] However, P. E. Razzell has argued that it was the decline in the deaths from small-pox (for medical reasons – inoculation) which caused the population growth after *c.* 1740; see his forthcoming 'Population Change in Eighteenth Century England: A Reinterpretation', *The Economic History Review*, 2nd series, XVIII, No. 2.　　　　　　　　[3] Deane and Cole, op. cit., Chapter III.

Increasing population meant an increasing labour force, and when this basic factor of production was better organized and equipped with better tools, total output certainly rose, and if wage rates are any indication, also *per capita* output.

IV

'Natura non facit saltum' [1]

This summary of the economic historians' theories about the origins of the industrial revolution, with a survey, with some help from the economists, of the 'forces making for growth' in the eighteenth century, has added little to our understanding of the industrial revolution. It has demonstrated only that the rise in eighteenth-century output was the result in part of improved organization and technology, and in part of expanding resources and the growth of population, without having explained the process of invention and its diffusion, or the reasons for the increase in population; it has stressed the importance for industrialization of a changing society and new social values, without explaining how those changes came about; it has demonstrated the need there was for a growing demand, particularly in the home market, without analysing how that demand grew and was sustained; it has argued that there was no great acceleration in capital formation as a prelude to, or as an accompaniment of the industrial revolution. The survey, moreover, has lead inevitably to the conclusion that the various 'forces making for growth' in the eighteenth century were not autonomous variables, but rather manifestations of growth itself; this seems to have been particularly true of capital accumulation, innovation, and population growth. Does this mean that changing human attitudes, in particular the development of a rational ethic about wealth, and the emergence of business enterprises motivated by profit-making (and, thus, the willingness to take risks), were the promoters of the industrial revolution? We cannot say; but, again, it is reasonable to argue that because the

[1] The motto of Alfred Marshall's *Principles of Economics* (London, 1890), which he translated as: 'economic evolution is gradual and continuous in each of its numberless routes'.

profit-motive depended on the possibility of making profits, this possibility was created by the economic changes of the eighteenth century. But do we need *an explanation* of the industrial revolution? Could it not be the culmination of a most un spectacular process, the consequence of a long period of slow economic growth?

In the policy writing about growth, two main conceptual models have been developed: the first, a sectoral model, in which a leading sector (or sectors) in a process of *unbalanced growth* activates the rest of the economy through backward linkages and technical diffusion;[1] the second, an aggregative model, in which, for example, the variation of a strategic variable, usually savings, has *general* impact throughout the economy, operating on a wide front on the aggregate capital-output ratio to produce *balanced growth*. The assumption today is that balanced growth, with simultaneous investment in all sectors of the economy, requires a plan and a strong government, but that unbalanced growth, 'the way that advanced countries of the Western world have in fact realized economic development',[2] is the natural outcome of a free-enterprise economy. But was England's development in the eighteenth century an example of unbalanced growth? Cannot the industrial revolution be explained more plausibly as the outcome of a process of balanced growth?[3] This growth was the product of long-term and widespread change in England: the rationalization of social attitudes; increasing knowledge and education; more and cheaper capital (the rate of interest had been falling from the early seventeenth century); greater factor flexibility and the more effective working of the price mechanism; widespread technical change (in both industry and agriculture); increasing factor supplies (population increase and more land –

---

[1] A. O. Hirschmann, *The Strategy of Economic Development* (Yale, 1958), has argued persuasively, and has made popular, the theory that economic imbalance is a stimulus to growth.

[2] S. Enke, *Economics for Development* (London, 1964), p. 332.

[3] It was Dr A. R. Hall (Australian National University) who, in a private communication ('Reflections on the Industrial Revolution'), convinced me that the industrial revolution could have been 'a consequence of a long period of slow economic growth'; he did not, however, base his argument explicitly on the 'balanced growth' thesis.

in America and at home, increasing raw material supplies) and fuller use of factors (fuller employment, less underemployment); better transport (which enabled, for example, trading in the winter months); the protection of infant industries (for example, silk and linen), which widened the industrial base of the economy.[1] There were also autonomous growth factors, for example the growth of foreign trade and the good harvests of the thirties and forties, whose impact was general. As the economy slowly expanded, so the market increased, giving incentive to the further division of labour and technical innovations, and to further growth. But what then becomes of the industrial revolution? What of the great discontinuity?

If one takes a long-term view of English economic development, say from 1700 to 1900 (or from 1750 to 1850, the traditional century of the industrial revolution), then it becomes obvious that there was in this period a radical shift in the structure of the economy, in the composition of total output, and in the distribution of employment, which gives concrete meaning to the idea of an industrial revolution. And in the rise of output central influence can be attributed to the great technical breakthroughs in industry of the period 1760–1800; it was these which allowed the acceleration of economic growth. Here perhaps the unbalanced growth concept helps. In the period *after* 1780 there were obvious growth sectors, sectors which were already important in the economy but which now grew faster, sectors with a large feed-back which triggered off quantity responses in other industries, as well as disseminating technical change widely. The cumulative effect was to produce a different type of economy in a relatively short period of time; this transformation the historians have called *The Industrial Revolution*. Given the previous growth of the economy, however, 'a turning-point' and 'a take-off' were certain when the pressure of demand on agriculture and industry was cumulatively great enough to stimulate a sufficient number of important technical changes which would enable a large and sustained increase in *per capita* output.

[1] Professor R. Davis has pointed out that tariffs became increasingly protective after 1690, so that by 1720 there was a fully protective system.

4 The Industrial Revolution and Economic Growth: The Evidence of Early British National Income Estimates[1]

P. DEANE

[This article was first published in *Economic Development and Cultural Change*, Vol. V, No. 1 (1957).]

For those concerned with problems of current economic policy in newly developing countries the lessons of past experience in industrialization have especial interest. A study of the early stages of economic growth whereby the industrialized countries of the world achieved their present relatively high standards of living might be expected to throw some light on the growth process itself. Unfortunately there is a great dearth of quantitative data on these early stages of industrialization. For most countries the statistical data required for an interpretation of the characteristic changes in industrial structure and standards of living do not begin to be available until the process is in full swing. The crucial initial stages which might throw some light on how and why the process began at all and what contributed to its acceleration or retardation when it was still in its infancy remain largely undocumented. The United Kingdom, as the first of the countries of the world to become highly industrialized, might be expected to provide a case history

[1] This article was written at the University of Cambridge Department of Applied Economics as part of an inquiry into the long-term economic growth of the United Kingdom which has been sponsored by the Committee on Economic Growth of the Social Science Research Council. It was originally published in Spanish in the *Bóletin del Banco Central de Venezuela*, No. 128–130, October–December 1955, and is reprinted here (in slightly revised form) by kind permission of the Banco Central de Venezuela. I am grateful to the Social Science Research Council for providing the funds necessary to carry out the research and to Professor Simon Kuznets in particular for constant advice and inspiration.

of peculiar interest. It is the purpose of this article to consider in particular the evidence of early British national income estimates in illuminating the process of the first industrial revolution.

It is generally accepted that the Industrial Revolution took place in Britain towards the end of the eighteenth century. That it had its roots deep in the past and that it initiated a continuous process of industrial change which is still not ended is also widely agreed. But there seems little doubt that towards the end of the eighteenth century Britain entered into a process of economic expansion which in character and pace was unlike anything previously experienced there or in any other country of the world. During the course of the nineteenth century Britain's Industrial Revolution spread to Western Europe and to Europe's overseas descendants in North America and Australia. In those countries which industrialized, real incomes rose with unprecedented rapidity and left the world average far behind. By 1949 according to calculations made by Professor Kuznets the inhabitants of the United States had average incomes which were more than six times the world average and in Western Europe it was more than twice the world average. For Latin America, on the other hand, *per capita* incomes were only about two-thirds of the world average and for Asia and Africa less than a quarter. The evidence suggests moreover that the gap between the industrialized countries and the unindustrialized countries of the world is still widening.[1]

ENGLAND BEFORE THE INDUSTRIAL REVOLUTION

In considering the genesis of this process of rapid industrialization, it is of some interest to study the characteristics of the

[1] These calculations on world incomes were made by Simon Kuznets on the basis of data in W. S. and E. S. Woytinsky, *World Population and Production*, New York, 1953 (for 1938 incomes) and in U.N. Statistical Office, 'National and *Per Capita* Incomes, Seventy Countries'. *Statistical Papers Series E*, No. 1, October 1950 (for 1949 incomes). The estimates were contained in the statistical appendix to 'Toward a Theory of Economic Growth', a paper given at Columbia University's Bicentennial Conference on 'National Policy for Economic Welfare at Home and Abroad' in May 1954.

economy which first gave rise to it. The material is incomplete. It is inevitable that the records of economic advance or decline should be more scanty for the pre-industrial phase of a country's history than for its period of industrialization. However, there exists for England at the end of the seventeenth century a set of national income estimates by Gregory King which give a picture of the economy as it was nearly a hundred years before the machine age began.[1] Table I presents a national product account derived from this source.

TABLE I *National Income and Expenditure of England and Wales in 1688 After Gregory King: in rounded percentages of the national income*

1. Income payments			3. Personal consumption	96
(a) Rents	27		4. Government expenditure	5
(b) Wages and salaries	37		5. Less indirect taxes	−6
(c) Profits, interest, and mixed income	36		6. Domestic asset formation	4
			7. Exports	10
			8. Less imports	−9
2. National income at factory cost		100	9. Expenditure of national income	100

It will be seen from Table I that by the end of the seventeenth century England had already developed a fairly complex exchange economy. Some idea of the extent to which specialization of labour had taken place can be seen from the fact that more than a third of the national income was distributed in the form of wages and salaries. In a highly industrialized economy the proportion attributable to compensation of employees is usually two-thirds or more and is certainly more than 50 per cent. But in very backward areas the proportion may be less than 10 per cent. This is true, for example, of present-day Nigeria or the Gold Coast: in Uganda it is about 19 per cent: and in Japan

[1] Gregory King's estimates, published in *Two Tracts by Gregory King*, George E. Barnett (ed.) (Baltimore, 1936), give most of the material for a set of social accounts for 1688. These accounts are set out and discussed in detail in my article on 'The Implications of Early National Income Estimates for the Measurement of Long-Term Economic Growth in the United Kingdom', *Economic Development and Cultural Change*, IV, No. 1 (November 1955).

the proportion seems to be about a half or rather less than a half.[1]

By the beginning of the eighteenth century, therefore, England was a country with a settled agriculture and a variety of handicrafts. More than half of its national income was derived from non-agricultural activities. King's estimates for the output of agriculture suggest that not much more than 40 per cent of national income was attributable to agriculture,[2] and an analysis of the trade statistics for the three years 1697–1701 has suggested that more than 80 per cent of English domestic exports were manufactured goods and more than 70 per cent of retained imports were foodstuffs and raw materials.[3] By contrast the proportion of national income attributable to the agriculture, forestry, and fishing group of industries in some underdeveloped countries, today is more than 50 per cent. In Nigeria, for example, it is about two-thirds and in India more than 50 per cent.

The statistical evidence that England had already achieved an appreciable level of economic development by the end of the seventeenth century is of course supported by more general data on its economic life. This was the Age of Reason in economic as well as in academic activities. More than a hundred new inventions were formally patented in the last decade of the century. In the same decade the Bank of England was founded and London already had a developed capital market.

That this development was a relatively slow process, however, is illustrated by the very low proportion of national income devoted to capital formation. It may be that the proportion of 4 per cent is an underestimate in that it omits corporate saving, but this could not have been an important fraction of

---

[1] See U.N. Statistical Office 'Statistics of National Income and Expenditure', *Statistical Papers Series H*, No. 8, 1955, for the data on the national income of present-day economies.

[2] Gregory King, op. cit., pp. 36–7.

[3] Ralph Davis, 'English Foreign Trade 1660–1770', *The Economic History Review*, 2nd Series VII, No. 2 (December 1954). These proportions are, of course, dependent on the system of classification adopted by Mr Davis and the line between semi-manufactured raw materials and manufactures is inevitably somewhat arbitrary. It should be noted, moreover, that most of the imported foodstuffs were manufactured or semi-manufactured commodities.

total saving at that time. King's estimates lend some support therefore to Professor Arthur Lewis's contention that the distinguishing mark of a backward economy is a rate of saving of only 4 or 5 per cent per annum.[1]

THE EARLY STAGES OF THE INDUSTRIAL REVOLUTION

At the beginning of the eighteenth century Britain's economy was probably almost stagnant. Within the next hundred years something happened to turn it into an expanding economy. Exactly when this happened it is difficult to say on the existing evidence though a more detailed analysis of trade and excise statistics might enable us to phase the process more adequately than is at present possible. The only general economic indices covering the whole century are the trade statistics at the official values (i.e. at constant prices). These are shown in Table II together with corresponding population figures.[2]

It will be seen from Table II that as far as the population figures are concerned the impression of stagnation lasts until the middle of the century. Then a persistent – and in some decades a very marked – expansion begins, accelerating towards the end of the century. Over the twenty years following 1741 the increase was at the rate of 5 per cent per decade; by the twenty years ending in 1811 it was at the rate of 12 per cent per decade. A similar picture of accelerating expansion emerges from the trade statistics though in these there is evidence of an improvement beginning before the middle of the century and a slump in the early seventeen-eighties. It is in the last two decades that the expansion appears to be sustained by forces of

[1] W. Arthur Lewis, *The Theory of Economic Growth* (London, 1955). See, for example, p. 225, where he says that: 'Communities in which the national income per head is not increasing invest 4 or 5 per cent of their national income per annum or less, while progressive communities invest 12 per cent or more.'

[2] The eighteenth-century population estimates are from John Brownlee 'History of the Birth and Death Rates in England and Wales', *Public Health*, June–July 1916. Trade figures are three-year averages centring on year specified, derived from the series published by contemporaries (Whitworth, Moreau, and Macpherson). They include re-exports. Being at official values, (i.e. largely at constant prices) they constitute a rough volume index of imports and exports respectively.

G

quite a different order to any that had emerged in earlier centuries. National income estimates made in 1770 by Arthur
Young suggest that agriculture still accounted for more than
40 per cent of the national income at that date but that manufactures accounted for 21 per cent.[1] Of this more than a third

TABLE 11   *English Population and Trade in the Eighteenth
Century*

	Population millions	Exports 3-year average £m.	Imports 3-year average £m.
1701	5·8	6·0	5·3
1711	6·0	6·4	4·4
1721	6·0	7·5	6·1
1731	5·9	8·4	7·3
1741	5·9	9·1	7·2
1751	6·1	12·6	7·9
1761	6·6	14·4	9·4
1771	7·1	15·9	12·8
1781	7·5	11·5	10·8
1791	8·2	21·3	17·7
1801	9·1	36·5	29·0

consisted of miscellaneous manufactures, including rural artisans
(blacksmiths, wheelwrights, etc.) mainly concerned with supplying agriculture.

By the time Young made his national income estimates, i.e. in
the seventies there had already been, according to his interpretation of events, a marked improvement in real incomes.[2] If we
accept his view we should date the beginning of rapid expansion from the fifties. In 1774 he wrote: 'Let any person consider
the progress of everything in Britain during the last twenty

[1] Arthur Young's estimates suggest 45 per cent as the proportion attributable
to agriculture. This is more than King's estimates suggest for 1688. There is no
doubt that Young tended to overestimate the value of agricultural output by
comparison in the other forms of economic activity but the possibility that the
relative contribution of agriculture actually increased between 1688 and 1770
should not be ruled out.

[2] Arthur Young, *Political Arithmetic, Part I* (London, 1774), p. 52. 'This better
living consists in the people consuming more food, and of a better sort: eating
wheat instead of barley, oats, and rye – and drinking a prodigiously greater
quantity of beer.'

years. The great improvements we have seen in this period, superior to those of another are not owing to the constitution, to moderate taxation or to other circumstances of equal efficacy ever since the Revolution, as the existence of these circumstances did not before produce equal effects. – The superiority has been owing to the quantity of wealth in the nation which has in a prodigious degree, facilitated the execution of all great works of improvement.'[1]

Young did not analyse the causes of the increase in wealth (which he seems to have regarded as equivalent to an increase of money in circulation) but he did describe its inflationary effects in making money easy to raise, in increasing demand and in raising prices.[2] If we look for the causes of this mid-century boom we may find some of them in the cumulative effect of an increased demand for English exports, already reflected in the trade figures by 1751 (see Table II) and of the unusually long run of good harvests which characterized the half-century following 1715.[3] Whatever the causes there seems to be good reason to suppose that there had been a distinct improvement in the economic environment by the middle decades of the century. Malthus wrote, for example, that: 'During the last forty years of the seventeenth century and the first twenty of the eighteenth, the average price of corn was such as, compared with the wages of labour, would enable the labourer to purchase, with a day's earnings, two thirds of a peck of wheat. From 1720 to 1750 the price of wheat had so fallen, while wages had risen, that instead of two thirds, the labourer could purchase the whole of a peck of wheat with a day's labour.'[4] Adam Smith took a similar view: 'In Great Britain the real

---

[1] Arthur Young, *Political Arithmetic*, p. 49.

[2] Op. cit., pp. 37 and 52 *et passim*.

[3] Cf. Thomas Tooke, *A History of Prices* (London, 1838), pp. 38–61. See, for example, p. 39: 'In this long interval of fifty years, there appear to have been only five seasons which, whether by inference from prices, or by historical notice could be considered as of a marked deficiency of produce or in any way approaching to what could be designated as seasons of scarcity.' And at p. 60: 'This long period of great abundance and consequent cheapness of the prices of provisions, was one which appears to have been attended with a great improvement in the condition and habits of the great bulk of the population.'

[4] T. R. Malthus, *Principles of Political Economy*, 2nd edn (London, 1836), p. 228.

recompence of labour, it has already been shown, the real quantities of the necessities and conveniences of life which are given to the labourer has increased considerably during the course of the present century.'[1] And again referring to the 'national progress of England towards wealth and improvement' he writes that: 'The annual produce of its land and labour is, undoubtedly, much greater at present than it was either at the restoration or the revolution.'[2]

In this favourable economic environment industrial inventions of which the textile inventions were the most numerous and spectacular in their immediate effects – flourished. By the end of the century industrialization was generating its own momentum. In 1744 it was still so feeble that Young, the champion of agriculture, wrote that he preferred an economic policy which encouraged industry and commerce rather than agriculture because 'trade and manufactures are children of more sickly and difficult growth; if you do not give them active encouragement they presently die'.[3] By 1814 Colquhoun was confident that 'the extensive capitals, skill and experience which British manufacturers have acquired' were such as to allay all fears or apprehension of any injurious competition in the foreign market, provided the improvements shall continue as heretofore to be progressive'.[4]

Between these two dates there had been a major change in the character and the direction of the British economy. The change in structure is reflected in the national income estimates suggested by Young's and Colquhoun's calculations respectively. Table III summarizes the estimates derivable from Young (for England and Wales) and from Colquhoun and later Pebrer

[1] Adam Smith, *The Wealth of Nations*, Modern Library (New York, 1937), p. 200.
[2] Ibid., p. 327. In this connexion cf. also the conclusion of Thomas McKeown and R. C. Brown in 'Medical Evidence Related to English Population Changes in the Eighteenth Century', *Population Studies*, IX, No. 2 (November 1955); that 'Improvements in the environment are therefore regarded as intrinsically the most acceptable explanation of the decline of mortality in the late eighteenth and nineteenth centuries.'
[3] Op. cit., p. 298.
[4] P. Colquhoun, *A Treatise on the Wealth, Power and Resources of the British Empire*, 2nd edn (London, 1815), p. 68.

(for the United Kingdom). They are very rough and they involve some arbitrary interpretations of estimates which the authors left inconsistent or inexplicit.[1] It is likely that the estimates based on Young somewhat overemphasize the contribution of agriculture and that the estimates based on Colquhoun understate the agricultural proportion. But even with these qualifications we should deduce that in this period the contribution of agriculture fell from over 40 per cent to under one-third and that the contribution of industry rose from about one-fifth to over one-quarter. By the later date factory industry was beginning to predominate over handicrafts and cotton had replaced wool as the major British industry.

An interesting feature of the estimates derived from Colquhoun is the relatively high proportion contributed by commerce (distribution, transport, and finance). If the three sets of estimates are reasonably consistent (and the Pebrer estimates were designed by their author to be consistent with Colquhoun's) this result implies a temporary increase in the share of commerce during the early stages of the Industrial Revolution. This is a hypothesis that requires further checking but it is conceivable that towards the end of the Napoleonic wars the merchant class was enjoying an abnormally high share of the national income and also that costs of transport and insurance were unusually high under war conditions. By 1831, it would appear from the estimates summarized in Table III that manufacture (including mines and building) accounted for more than a third of national income and also that the industrial basis of the economy had broadened considerably. Apparently mines and mineral manufactures accounted for more than 4 per cent of the national income in 1831 compared with about 2 per cent in 1812; and hardware accounted for over 3 per cent according

[1] See my article on 'The Implications of Early National Income Estimates, etc.' for a more extended discussion of Young's and Colquhoun's estimates and the adjustments required to make them conceptually consistent and complete. See also Phyllis Deane, 'Contemporary Estimates of National Income in the Nineteenth Century, I', *The Economic History Review*, VIII, No. 3 (April 1956), where estimates are derived from Colquhoun for Great Britain only: these suggest about 25 per cent for the contribution of agriculture and over 30 per cent for manufacture.

to the 1831 estimates whereas in 1812 they had been valued at only about 1½ per cent. By 1831, according to Pebrer, the iron industry accounted for about a fifth of the value of mines and mineral manufactures, and was worth four times the value put upon it by Colquhoun for 1812. Since Young made his estimates, the output of pig-iron had probably increased more than tenfold.[1]

TABLE III   *The Structure of National Income 1770–1831*
As percentages of the total national income

	1770 England and Wales (After Young)	1812 United Kingdom (After Colquhoun)	1831 United Kingdom (After Pebrer)
Agriculture	45	27	28
Manufacture (including mines and building)			
Wool	4	4½	3
Leather	3	3	3
Flax, hemp, glass, earthenware	1½	4½	3
Cotton and silk	1½	6	7
All other	11	12	19
Commerce	13	20	15
Miscellaneous other	21	23	22

Sources: Estimates for 1770 from Arthur Young, *Political Arithmetic*, Part II (London, 1779); and *Northern Tour* (1770). Estimates for 1812 from P. Colquhoun, *A Treatise on the Wealth, Power and Resources of the British Empire* (London, 1815). Estimates for 1831 from P. Pebrer, *Taxation, Expenditure, Power, Statistics and Debt of the Whole British Empire* (London, 1833). But see my article on 'The Implications of Early National Income Estimates, etc.' and 'Contemporary Estimates of National Income in the Nineteenth Century' for details of the way in which the estimates were built up from these sources.

If we consider what was happening to the level of incomes in the early stages of the Industrial Revolution we find that the evidence is scanty and imprecise. That there was some increase in real incomes during the first six or seven decades of the century seems fairly certain. The passage quoted above from Malthus implies that in terms of their potential wheat purchase, average real incomes of labourers increased by about 50 per

[1] H. Scrivenor, *History of the Iron Trade* (London, 1854), gives estimates of 17,350 tons for the output of pig-iron in 1740; 68,300 tons for 1788; and 678,417 for 1830.

cent. A comparison of Young's and King's estimates suggests that average real incomes rather more than doubled between 1688 and 1770. There appears to have been no other considered estimate of national income made between these dates although a broadsheet by Joseph Massie gave average income estimates for different classes of the community and made calculations containing implicit estimates of the numbers in each class.[1] Massie's calculations were made in an attempt to expose the exorbitant gains of the owners of sugar plantations rather than with the design of estimating aggregate incomes either for particular classes or for the nation as a whole. His estimates of average income were in no way essential to his main argument and it would be unwise to assume that he had considered them at all carefully. However, for what they are worth they suggest an average income of about £42 per family or about 30 per cent above King's estimate of £32 at a slightly higher level of prices. Massie did not estimate total population so that we cannot convert his data to a per head basis.

Table IV summarizes the estimates of average national income available for four points of time – in 1688 about a century before the Industrial Revolution is generally thought to have begun, in 1770 just before the first great textile inventions and the steam engine were patented, and 1800 and 1812 when the process of industrialization had certainly begun. The estimate for 1812 is for Great Britain rather than England and Wales and is accordingly slightly lower than the comparable English average.

As has already been emphasized these national income estimates are extremely rough and cannot be used to support any precise quantitative analysis. In particular the Young estimates

---

[1] Massie's estimates of 'annual incomes or expenses', 'money exorbitantly raised on each family', and 'money exorbitantly raised in all families' are contained in a broadsheet entitled *A Computation of the Money that hath been Exorbitantly Raised upon the People of Great Britain by the Sugar Plantations in One Year from January, 1759 to January 1760*. The classes apparently correspond to those distinguished by King but a comparison of the averages for each class suggest that there were unexplained differences in definition and a study of the distribution of incomes implicit in Massie's calculations throws a doubt on the internal consistency of his estimates.

on which the 1770 figure is based are probably overestimates. Moreover, the price indicators constitute a very unsatisfactory reflection of changes in the value of money. But in spite of the qualifications that are necessary in interpreting these estimates the most interesting feature of the evidence remains unaltered.

TABLE IV *Estimates of Average National Income Derived from Contemporary Sources 1688–1812*

Year	Population	Average money National income	Price indicators for consumer goods. Five year averages based on the Gilboy–Schumpeter index $1700-1 = 100$
England and Wales			
1688	5·5	8·7	99
1770	7·0	18·5	108
1800	9·1	21·9	186
Great Britain			
1812	12·3	26·8	172

Sources: For the national income estimates see 'The Implications of Early National Income Estimates, etc.' and 'Contemporary Estimates of National Income in the Nineteenth Century'. For the basic price index see E. B. Schumpeter: 'English Prices and Public Finance, 1660–1822', *Review of Economic Statistics*, xx, No. 1 (February 1938); the figures in this table are five year averages centring on the year specified. The pre-1800 population estimates are Brownlee's estimates, op. cit.: from 1801 onward Census of Population data were available.

It suggests that most, if not all, of the advance in average real incomes which had been achieved between the end of the seventeenth and the beginning of the nineteenth century had been achieved by 1770, *before* the Industrial Revolution had well begun. In the last three decades of the eighteenth century, that is in the period which saw the unmistakable beginnings of rapid industrialization the rate of increase in average real incomes was apparently negligible, if indeed there was not a positive decline.

Much more research will be necessary before we can measure actual rates of growth or decline for this period. The evidence strongly suggests, however, that the beginning of industrialization in Britain followed a period of rising real incomes and was accompanied by a phase of falling or stagnating incomes. It would seem as if a long period of good harvests and expanding foreign markets precipitated an expansion of population and industry during which the growth in total output was insufficient to keep pace with the rise in population and the rise in money incomes was nullified by the fall in the value of money.

This is not to deny that the British economy was expanding at a faster rate under the impulse of industrialization than it had ever done before. The volume of foreign trade per head of the population (imports plus domestic exports at official values) apparently increased by an average of about 13 per cent per decade in the four decades before 1760 and by about 17 per cent in the last four decades of the century. Before 1720 the rate of increase was not more than about 5 per cent per decade. Domestic exports per head actually rose at a somewhat faster rate in the four decades before 1760 than in the four following decades.

In absolute terms and in particular branches of manufacture, however, the expansion accelerated to a remarkable extent towards the end of the eighteenth century. The growing industries – of which the textile industries were the leaders – entered into a new phase of expansion in the seventeen-eighties. The cotton industry, which was the most spectacular example, expanded its imports of raw material tenfold in three decades. Printed goods charged to duty in the decade ending in 1779. Other industries followed at a more modest pace but for most of these for which data are available the general quickening was unmistakable.[1] For tallow candles, for soap, for coal shipments into London, and for British spirits and strong beer, for example, the 1790–99 averages were all between a quarter and a half above the 1770–79 averages. By the beginning of the nineteenth century the output of British industry was probably 50 per cent to 100 per cent above its volume in 1770.

---

[1] Cf. Walther G. Hoffmann, *British Industry 1700–1950* (London, 1955). Hoffmann's index suggests that the real value of industrial output roughly doubled in the last thirty years of the century. For this period his index was almost entirely based on data for the textile industries and on London's receipts of coal; and the rate of growth for all industry was probably less than these series would suggest.

This was certainly a remarkable rate of increase but industry probably accounted for no more than a quarter of the total national income by the end of the eighteenth century. Meanwhile the 1801 population was some 30 per cent above the 1771 population and the proportion of adults was probably falling.[1] Only if there had been a substantial increase in the productivity of non-industrial activities – and particularly of agricultural and commercial activities – could this expansion of population and industry have been accompanied by an appreciable improvement in average real incomes.

Another factor which may have put some brake on the rate of economic growth in the early decades of the Industrial Revolution was the effect of the Revolutionary and Napoleonic wars. The evidence on this point is by no means conclusive but it seems fairly certain that war was a retarding factor. According to Hoffman: 'The period 1793–1817 may be regarded as a break in a period of particularly rapid industrialization.'[2] A contemporary observer looking back over the war period took the view that the average level of real incomes rose at the commencement of the war, stagnated during its second half, and fell sharply during the post-war period.[3]

If there was no great improvement in the average standard of living during the early stages of British industrialization there were important changes for some sections of the community. The skilled and semi-skilled operatives in the new factories found their money incomes rising – sometimes faster than the level of prices. There were full-time jobs in factories for many women and children who formerly had few opportunities of adding to the family income except in seasonal agricultural labour or irregular domestic spinning. For workers who were

[1] Cf. T. H. Marshall, 'The Population Problem During the Industrial Revolution', E. M. Carus-Wilson (ed.), in *Essays in Economic History* (London, 1954), p. 321. We know that population began to increase rapidly about 1780 and continued to do so, at an accelerating pace, till 1820, with a high birth-rate and a falling death-rate, particularly among infants.

[2] W. G. Hoffmann, op. cit., p. 32.

[3] Joseph Lowe, *The Present State of England* (London, 1822). See 'Contemporary Estimates of National Income in the Nineteenth Century' for a discussion of Lowe's analysis and its relation to other estimates and assessments for the period.

displaced by machines on the other hand and for peasant farmers squeezed by enclosure into the position of day-labourers employment was often difficult to obtain and earnings lagged behind the rising cost of provisions. In effect there was a considerable change in the distribution of incomes both as between industries and occupations[1] and as between different classes of society.

There seems also to have been a perceptible increase in the inequality of incomes since before the Industrial Revolution. King's estimates of the average earnings of different social classes suggest that in 1688, 92 per cent of the families (i.e. families earning £50 and less) earned 63 per cent of total incomes. According to a similar set of estimates made by Colquhoun for 1803, 92 per cent of the families (i.e. families earning £150 and under) earned 56 per cent of total incomes.[2] A comparison of the results class by class confirms this impression that the rich had grown relatively richer and the poor relatively poorer over this period, though the evidence does not indicate whether the change occurred after rapid industrialization began, or in the first six or seven decades of the eighteenth century.[3]

In sum, therefore, it would seem that the early stages of the industrialization of Britain were characterized by important changes in the structure of the national product and a rate of population growth which outstripped the growth of real output. It is possible that the average standard of living actually fell during this phase. Probably also there was an increase in the inequality of incomes accompanying large shifts in the distribution as between industries and occupations and still other shifts as between types of income-receiver which were a

---

[1] Cf. T. S. Ashton, *An Economic History of England: The 18th Century* (London, 1955), p. 234. 'It would seem that the difference in pay between skilled and unskilled increases', and p. 235, 'The divergence of experience between skilled and less skilled explains how honest observers could differ as to whether things were getting better or worse for labour at this time.'

[2] P. Colquhoun, *Treatise on Indigence* (London, 1806), p. 23.

[3] Massie's estimates, op. cit. ought to give some indication of this but are unsatisfactory. They give a somewhat implausible picture of the income distribution in 1759 and suggest that the lower 92 per cent (i.e. those families earning under £100) received only 45 per cent of total incomes.

consequence of the war-induced inflation. It seems likely also that war and immediately post-war dislocations in agricultural and commercial activities prevented industrialization from proceeding as rapidly as it might otherwise have done during the first two decades of the nineteenth century.

5 The Supply of Raw Materials in the Industrial Revolution

E. A. WRIGLEY

[This article was first published in *The Economic History Review*, 2nd series, Vol. XV, No. 1 (1962).]

Any great increase in the output of industry, such as began in England towards the end of the eighteenth century, must have as its counterpart an equally great increase in the input of industrial raw materials at the other end of the process of production.[1] The problem of providing an adequate raw material supply had been acute in many branches of industry in earlier centuries. The removal of these constrictions is intimately connected with several important aspects of the rapid growth which occurred, and its study affords a vantage point from which they can conveniently be surveyed.

The most important change in raw material provision which took place was the substitution of inorganic for organic sources of supply, of mineral for vegetable or animal raw materials. This was a *sine qua non* of sustained industrial growth on a large scale, for when industrial growth is based upon vegetable and animal raw materials present success can usually be obtained only at the cost of future difficulties. England in the sixteenth and seventeenth centuries provides some typical examples of the dilemma which confronts industries when they use animal or vegetable raw materials. The iron industry of the Weald was able to expand without prejudice to its future prosperity only up to the point at which the annual cut of timber equalled the yearly increment of new growth. Any expansion beyond this point could take place only at the cost of contraction in the

---

[1] Except, of course, in so far as technological changes permit raw material saving.

future. Expansion without prejudice to future supplies could, of course, have been secured if more land had been devoted to the production of timber, but in a country where the area of unused land was small more woodland meant less ploughland or pasture. Competition for the use of scarce land was a perennial problem in these circumstances and a permanent, radical increase of industrial, raw material supply was very difficult to obtain. Those Tudor pamphleteers who complained that the sheep were eating up men were directing attention to the central problem of industrial raw material supply in an age when organic materials were essential for most industrial processes. More land devoted to the production of timber or wool meant less land available to produce food. The price of raw materials was sure to rise because of competition for the use of land and so inhibit industrial growth even where the government refrained from direct political action to guarantee the supply of food. If the government did not intervene to restrict pasture in the interest of tillage, the play of the market would ultimately produce the same result. Moreover, industrial growth not only provoked problems of this type directly by competing for the use of land, but also indirectly by encouraging a growth in population which in turn increased the demand for land upon which food could be grown. Once the spread of settlement had brought all available land into use, the only way in which the supply of food and of industrial raw materials of vegetable or animal origin could be increased simultaneously was by a general rise in the productivity of the land.[1]

The view that the productivity of the land controls the growth of industry no less than that of agriculture is a recurring theme in the *Wealth of Nations*. Adam Smith wrote just before the dramatic changes in industrial raw material supply had become fully apparent and did not recognize their importance. In his chapter *Of the natural Progress of Opulence* he began by defining the exchange of products manufactured in the towns

---

[1] Within any one national market area, of course, it was possible to expand the supply of food and raw materials without increasing pressure on the land by import from abroad. Cheap sea transport enabled England to make good some of her shortage of timber, for example, in this fashion.

for agricultural produce and raw materials as 'the great commerce of every civilized society'.[1] Later in the chapter he enlarged upon the nature of this exchange.

> It is this commerce which supplies the inhabitants of the town, both with the materials of their work, and the means of their subsistence. The quantity of the finished work which they sell to the inhabitants of the country, necessarily regulates the quantity of the materials and provisions which they buy. Neither their employment nor subsistence, therefore, can augment, but in proportion to the augmentation of the demand from the country for finished work; and this demand can augment only in proportion to the extension of improvement and cultivation. Had human institutions, therefore, never disturbed the natural course of things, the progressive wealth and increase of the towns would, in every political society, be consequential, and in proportion to the improvement and cultivation of the territory or country.[2]

If the productivity of the land in the last analysis governed the wealth of any country, it is hardly surprising that Adam Smith claimed of investment in agriculture that 'Of all the ways in which a capital can be employed, it is by far the most advantageous to society'.[3]

The supply of mineral raw materials forms an interesting contrast with the supply of vegetable and animal raw materials. In the very long run the mineral supply problem is insoluble in a sense which is not true of organic raw materials, since every mine is a wasting asset. It cannot be made to give a sustained yield in the way which is possible with a forest or a farm. A forest can yield indefinitely: a mine cannot. Nevertheless, in any but the very long run the difficulty of obtaining a large increase in supply is less pronounced with mineral raw materials. Given an adequate mining technique and the existence of rich deposits production can rapidly be built up to high levels. As the

[1] A. Smith, *An Inquiry into the Nature and Causes of the Wealth of Nations*, J. R. McCulloch (ed.) (Edinburgh, 1828), II, p. 171.
[2] Ibid., pp. 175–6.   [3] Ibid., p. 150.

individual mine nears exhaustion the price of extraction must rise, of course, but as long as it is possible to sink other pits to tap equally rich deposits the price of the product need not rise, and may well fall if increasing production encourages the creation of larger and more efficient production units. Moreover, an increase in the production of mineral raw materials does not take place at the expense of the supply of food or of other industrial raw materials. There is no equivalent in the production of inorganic raw materials to the competition for land which accompanies an expansion in the production of organic raw materials.[1] In the half century after the publication of the *Wealth of Nations* the vital importance of the new sources of industrial raw materials became clear. The passage which McCulloch in his edition found 'perhaps the most objectionable'[2] in the book was that which concluded that capital was best employed in agriculture from the point of view of society as a whole. Adam Smith had argued that rent is created by those 'powers of nature' which give an added productivity to agriculture, but had added that in manufacture nature does nothing for man; he must do everything for himself. McCulloch objected to this definition of rent, but he also denied that the powers of nature favoured agriculture alone. His was a world in which the importance of manufacture had ceased to be regulated solely by agricultural productivity. The amount of capital which could profitably be invested in manufacture was no longer controlled by the agricultural surplus in the manner suggested by Adam Smith.[3] Mineral sources of raw material had given another dimension to the discussion. To McCulloch the 'powers of nature' revealed in the steam engine were as remarkable as any that Adam Smith had noticed in the fields.[4]

[1] Open-cast mining forms a minor exception to this rule.

[2] Smith, *Wealth of Nations*, ii, p. 150 n.

[3] See, for example, *Wealth of Nations*, ii, pp. 214–15, where his argument leads him to the conclusion that the manufactures of Leeds, Halifax, Sheffield, Birmingham, and Wolverhampton are 'the offspring of agriculture'. The general argument of the chapter *Of the different Employment of Capitals* is also interesting in this connexion.

[4] '. . . are not the pressure of the atmosphere and the elasticity of steam, which enable us to work the most stupendous engines, the spontaneous gifts of nature?' *Wealth of Nations*, ii, p. 150 n.

There is a second difference of great importance between mineral production on the one hand, and vegetable and animal production on the other. Production of the former is puncti-form; of the latter areal. The transport problems involved in moving a million tons of coal from pitheads scattered over an area of only a few square miles are quite different from those involved in moving the same weight of grain or timber from an area of several thousands of square miles. The former implies heavy tonnages moving along a small number of routeways, whereas the latter implies the reverse. A heavy capital invest-ment in improved communications is unlikely to give a good return when the raw materials of industry are organic since the traffic density along any one route is usually low. A large volume of mineral traffic, on the other hand, makes such an investment necessary to cope with physical difficulties, and financially attractive because the total possible savings are so much greater.[1]

I

The decisive technological change which freed so many in-dustries from dependence upon organic raw materials was the discovery of a way of using coal where once wood had been essential. The timing of the change varied a great deal between the several industries. It came earliest in industries like the boiling of salt in which the use of coal presented no problem of undesired chemical change in the product because the source of heat was separated from the object by a sheet of metal. Industries like iron smelting and hop drying in which contact was more intimate presented greater problems in a period when chemical knowledge was slight. A long period of trial and error commonly elapsed before a successful method of substitution was developed. Coal-fired salt pans were a commonplace before the end of the sixteenth century: coke-fired blast furnaces were

[1] Occasionally the older system had coped with quite heavy tonnages. The grain and timber trade, especially to the London market, was on a substantial scale and had meant large outlays on North Sea and coastal shipping and on river barges, but it was the new problems of mineral traffic on a large scale which pro-duced the canals and the railways.

H

not successfully operated until the first quarter of the eighteenth, and in some branches of the iron industry it was near to the end of the century before charcoal could be dispensed with. In spite of the rather slow spread of coal use from one industry or process to another, however, it was already an industrial raw material of the first importance by the beginning of the eighteenth century. At that time coal production in England and Wales had reached a level of about 3 million tons per annum, or roughly half a ton per head of population. The production of coal both absolutely and *per caput* was already of quite a different order of magnitude in England from that obtaining on the continent; and by the end of the century production had tripled. Much of the coal was used for domestic rather than industrial purposes, but all helped to relieve the pressure on timber supplies. Wherever it could successfully be substituted for wood its effect was to liberate production from the physical limits upon output imposed on industries requiring a source of heat in a country where the timber resources were very limited. Unlike timber, a substantial increase in coal consumption in any one period did not prejudice supplies in the next, nor did an expansion in coal use in one industry affect others adversely. Moreover, once the initial period of prejudice against coal had passed and the difficulties involved in its use had been overcome, many industries discovered that coal was better suited to their purposes than wood had been.

In the absence of coal the timber requirements of a country whose industries were as large as those of England at the beginning of the nineteenth century would have been enormous. Much heat was needed in a wide range of industrial processes, and to have provided it with wood must have denuded the forests of England, indeed the forests of Europe, in a few decades. The classic case is perhaps that of the iron industry. Benaerts quotes an estimate, for example, that the production of 10,000 tons of charcoal iron required the felling of 40,000 hectares of forest.[1] The pig which resulted from a coal or coke melt was for many years unsatisfactory and commanded only

---

[1] P. Benaerts, *Les Origines de la grande industrie allemande* (Paris, 1933), p. 454. One hectare is equal to 2½ acres.

a very low price. The prejudice against it remained for some time even after Darby had overcome the main difficulties in smelting ore with coke, yet coke pig was to prove essential to the rapid progress of industrial growth. Without it there could have been no great expansion in the scale of iron output or fall in its price, and the physical properties of iron were so essential to the age of machines that it is difficult to believe that any great changes were possible without cheap and abundant iron. Many machines which were first constructed in wood could be greatly improved when made in metal, and many of the great engineering constructions after the turn of the century could not have been made at all without cheap iron. The physical properties of iron permit great precision of working: the steam engine and the machine tool depend on this. They and the iron ships, iron rails and iron bridges of the new age required the successful supplanting of vegetable by mineral fuels.

Coal could not be used as a direct substitute for wood in the building industry where timber was used not as a fuel but as a building material, but indirectly it was important because its use in the brick industry meant that the production of bricks could be expanded without unit costs of production rising, so that brick became the prime building material of the new age. The engineering and construction industries, as producer goods industries of central importance, are points of great sensitivity in any period of rapid industrial growth. The output of producer goods must necessarily expand faster than that of consumer goods at such a time, and it is vital that it should be easily expansible, and if possible that the costs of the raw materials involved should show a secular tendency to fall as the volume of production increases. In the past these industries had been heavily dependent on wood, which tended to induce a secular rise in the costs of the raw material when the scale of production grew. After the changeover to mineral raw materials the possibility of a much easier and unrestricted expansion was always present.

Those consumer goods industries, such as the Staffordshire pottery industry or the glass industry, which required much heat in their manufacturing processes also benefited from growing independence of vegetable fuel. Brewing, the paper industry, and some sections of the textile industry made use of coal too, though in their case the fuel was used to process organic rather than inorganic raw materials.

A part of the great increase in the productivity of industrial workers which began in the later part of the eighteenth century and has continued down to the present day arose in the manner which Adam Smith described and analysed. Markets grew larger; production processes were subdivided; industrial skills became more specialized and workers nicer in their skills; new machinery was developed; real costs fell as productivity increased. But a part of the increase in productivity which took place, that part which became possible as a result of the rise to prominence of a class of industrial raw materials whose significance Adam Smith did not fully appreciate, that part which arose from cheaper and more abundant heat and mechanical power, could not take place as long as the land produced not merely the food of the nation but also its industrial raw materials. It is notable how frequently the industries in which expansion was marked in the years between Adam Smith and McCulloch were those which were gradually freeing themselves from dependence upon organic raw materials, especially wood. This is true of the industries making iron, non-ferrous metals, most types of machinery, glass, salt, pottery, and bricks. The industry in which the most dramatic growth of all took place was, perhaps, cotton which provides an instructive contrast with most other quickly growing industries in that its raw material was vegetable. The cotton industry conformed quite closely to the picture of industrial growth envisaged by Adam Smith and will require further consideration at a later stage in this discussion.

II

Though the large-scale use of coal offered great opportunities, it also brought problems, in whose solution may be seen some of the most important economic and technological foundations of the Industrial Revolution. The prime difficulty was the great expense of transporting coal with the existing transport media. Coal could only come into general domestic and industrial use if it were cheap, and could only be cheap if it could be cheaply transported. As long as the price of coal taken overland doubled within five miles of the pithead it was not likely to be widely used. This, of course, is the reason why the first large-scale coal industry was on the Tyne in touch by sea with the London market and the smaller markets down the east coast. Sea transport had always been the cheapest form of transport, and moreover it had long been accustomed to dealing with the range of problems raised by punctiform production on a large scale. Large ports had for centuries concentrated a great bulk of goods at a single point and forwarded them to a limited number of similar points, often far away. The biggest ships were capable of moving hundreds of tons at a time, whereas on land loads measured by the hundredweight were normal. Exceptionally much larger weights might be moved (as with large building stones), but only over short distances and by making special arrangements. Before the era of large-scale mineral production there was little incentive to try to alter the capacity of overland transport systems since the areal production of vegetable and animal products seldom calls for the movement of a great bulk of material along a single route. Improvements to overland transport which are precluded when raw material production is areal may be both necessary and economically practicable when raw material production is punctiform. Once the Newcastle–London coal trade had shown the very real advantages of coal over wood for many purposes there was always latent the possibility that a radical improvement in overland communication might take place.

Prof. Nef has shown how important the growth of the coal trade was in developing more efficient methods of ship construction and working in this country.[1] By the end of the seventeenth century about half of the total British merchant fleet by tonnage was engaged in the coal trade. But the effect of the development of large-scale punctiform mineral production upon shipping was only to develop traits characteristic of the

[1] J. U. Nef, *The Rise of the British Coal Industry* (1932), I, pp. 238–40, 390–4.

movement of goods by sea for a long time. Ports and pits had much in common as sources of cargo. It was otherwise with overland transport. When the production of the coal industry came to be measured in hundreds of thousands and even millions of tons annually a new solution was necessary if the coal was to reach inland centres of consumption. However inefficient to later eyes may have been the movement of grain, wood, and wool on horseback or in carts along pitted roads, it was economically inevitable since the volume of the traffic was too small to warrant the investment needed to provide good roads or canals. Areal production meant poor communications. Minerals had, of course, also been moved on horseback before the eighteenth century in spite of the punctiform nature of their production, but they had moved in quite small absolute quantities and had not afforded any opportunity for substantial improvement. For a long time coal was moved in the same way whenever it was moved overland. It moved on pack animals from the Staffordshire coalfield to the Northwich salt pans and from the Yorkshire pits to the Bradford dyers, or on small river craft on the Severn and Thames. As long as the inland consumption of coal remained small, coal moved as other raw materials had moved for centuries. Large-scale consumption provided new opportunities. The demonstration that coal could be used so successfully where wood had been used in the past created a large potential demand for it which could not be met while communications were poor, but which provided a powerful incentive to improve them. The canalization of the Weaver to Northwich after 1720 in order to provide cheaper coal than could be brought overland from Staffordshire was an early example of the improvements in transport encouraged by the use of coal; and the work done on the Douglas from Wigan to the Ribble estuary dates from the same period. As coal consumption rose, more ambitious works became possible. Waterways were not merely improved; they were created. Forty years after the work on the Weaver and the Douglas the Worsley Canal was built, to be followed by many others in the next half century.

The art of building canals was not new to Europe. The Dutch

had a long experience of making them, and several long canals were built in France in the seventeenth century, but the English canal network was constructed in response to an incentive of a new type. If mineral raw materials were to continue to grow in importance in English industry they required such a network. Canals are well suited to the movement of goods produced at a point, but not to areal production. The truth of this is well illustrated by the history of the many canals which were built in the first flush of enthusiasm for canals in purely agricultural areas of the country, and which were seldom successful financially.[1] The successful canals were those on which there was a heavy volume of mineral traffic, usually coal, but occasionally other minerals also: for example, the canal from the pottery district of Staffordshire to the Mersey carried a china clay traffic. Agricultural areas through which the canals passed benefited greatly from their presence, both because they made possible much cheaper movement of food to the market and because some of the essentials of good husbandry, such as lime and manure, were more easily obtainable after their construction. Agricultural traffic contributed significantly to the revenues of many canals built to cater chiefly for mineral traffic, but agricultural traffic was characteristically insufficient to sustain canal finances on its own, and canals which were built in agricultural areas in the hope that their presence would create sufficient traffic to make them profitable seldom fulfilled their promoters' expectations.

The development of railways, the other chief means of cheap internal transport created during the Industrial Revolution, was also closely connected with the switch to inorganic raw materials, and especially the transport of coal. From the seventeenth century there had been railways connecting pitheads with coal wharves on the Tyne, developed to deal with the problem of coal movement overland on a large scale. The laying of wooden planks along which the horse-drawn carts could move was a simple way of increasing the load which each horse

---

[1] Clapham noted this condition, though he cast his conclusions about it in a different form. J. H. Clapham, *An Economic History of Modern Britain* (2nd edn, Cambridge, 1950), I, p. 82.

could shift. When he no longer had to expend most of his energy in overcoming the mud in wet weather and the deep ruts in dry, a horse drawing a cart along planked ways was able to move two or three times as much coal. Once the volume of coal moving over the short roads to the wharves had become large the heavy expense of improving roads in this way proved well worthwhile. In time flanged wheels were introduced and it became profitable to cover the wooden tracks with metal plates in order to increase their life under constant heavy usage. Railways were peculiarly a mining development (even down to the track gauge), and were created to overcome the problems posed by large-scale punctiform mineral production, initially as feeders to waterways, but later as an independent network. Like canals, they also, of course, proved in time of great benefit to other forms of production and made easier the movement of the vegetable and animal raw materials. Moreover, they developed a great passenger traffic. Yet it is true of railways as of canals that most of those built in purely agricultural areas in England did not generate enough traffic to make them profitable.

As the eighteenth century progressed the volume of coal output rose steadily, from 3 million tons at the beginning to about 10 millions at the end. The great coalfields near Newcastle no longer grew in output as quickly as some of the inland fields because the improvement in communications, especially the development of canals, made available to industrial and domestic consumers over a steadily increasing area the advantages which during the seventeenth century had been restricted to the east coast ports and to very small areas on the inland fields. Even at the beginning of the century probably no other mineral, vegetable, or animal raw material approached coal in weight of production: by the end it had far outdistanced any rival. It was therefore peculiarly coal which provided at once the chief stimulus to the building of traffic arteries capable of dealing with the quantities of raw materials now used by the economy, and the main goods traffic on the canals and later the railways.[1]

[1] Paradoxically, although so many of the most important changes in transport and power were connected with the mining industry and specially coal, and

III

Or the issue may be put in different terms. The importance of the changes in raw material supply and in the transport system can be illustrated from the writings of the economists of the period as well as traced in the narrative economic history, especially in the discussions of the limits of economic growth. The starkest discussion of the organization of economic life in a society bounded by the productivity of the land and the problems of transport is perhaps that of Thünen. When Thünen published his discussion of the pattern of land use which would be found upon a featureless plain surrounding a central city, he deliberately made a limited number of simple assumptions about the nature of its economic life. Upon these assumptions he was able to show that the steady rise in the cost of transporting produce as distance increased from the central market would cause the land to be divided up into a series of concentric rings each marked by a different type of land use. The innermost ring was devoted to the production of perishable commodities like milk and vegetables; the next ring to woodland to meet the city's need for fuel, charcoal, building materials, tools, and furniture; and the remaining rings to agriculture of a gradually decreasing intensity, shelving off finally into pastoral activities at the point where the cost of transporting grain to the market made it unprofitable to plough and plant the land. Everything depended upon the demand in the central market, local changes in agricultural productivity, and the level of transport

---

although it was the adoption of mineral raw materials generally in industry which alone made possible the scale of expansion which occurred, the mining industry itself did not experience any revolutionary increase in manpower productivity. Output per man-year in a large coal pit in 1700 was about 150 tons (Nef, *The Rise of the British Coal Industry*, 11, pp. 136 n.), a figure already about two-fifths as large as the peak figure in the 1880s. The coal industry, indeed, is sometimes referred to as an example of the impossibility of designing machines to perform all jobs previously done by hand, and is classed with, say, agriculture, in this respect. But the central difficulty of the production of coal has never been the winning of coal at the coal-face, hard and dangerous though this has always been, but its transport within the pit, up the pit shaft, and from the pithead to the point of consumption. The canal and the steam engine solved the prime difficulties of the coal mines. Those at the coal-face were less pressing.

charges. As the price of raw materials and food rose in the central market, for example, or alternatively as the cost of transport fell, the whole system of rings would expand allowing a larger area of land to be used more intensively. Thünen himself illustrated the dramatic effect of falling transport costs on the intensity of land use by examining the effect of a river running across the series of rings to the central city along which transport costs were only a tenth of those overland. Thünen's model underlined many of the characteristics of the economic life of earlier centuries. His scheme makes it clear how crippling the high cost of transport can be; how, for example, local famine might well occur in a country enjoying a general sufficiency; how, though timber was essential to such an economy, its great bulk and weight made it difficult to deliver to a market at a reasonable low cost. When he published his book in 1826 his model still fitted the economic life of parts of Germany without excessive distortion, though by that date it was no longer appropriate to England. Thünen acknowledged Adam Smith as his chief mentor,[1] but his scheme embodied only a part of the world Adam Smith had studied. The *Wealth of Nations* describes a much more complicated world; it does not merely abstract from it some of its salient characteristics as *Der isolirte Staat* had done. Although Adam Smith maintained that a gradual rise in agricultural productivity alone made possible the development of cities and industry, and further maintained that in the last resort the size and wealth of cities must continue to be governed by the productivity of the land, he understood and entertained within his scheme of analysis the great modification and complication which arose out of the development of trade between city and city and nation and nation, not restricting himself simply to the consideration of trade between a city and its surrounding countryside. The wealth of nations could increase greatly when Thünen's limiting assumptions were relaxed in this way, and Adam Smith showed clearly how this might come about, and discussed which policies were likely to expedite the process or

---

[1] J. V. v. Thünen, *Der isolirte Staat in Beziehung auf Landwirtschaft und Nationalökonomie* (2nd edn, Rostock, 1842–50), Part II, p. 1.

to frustrate it. The wealth of nations could not, however, increase without limit upon the assumptions within which Adam Smith worked since the productivity of the land set a ceiling to growth. In the half-century following the course of events proved beyond doubt that the assumptions might be still further relaxed. The ceiling which Adam Smith had assumed to exist generally now applied only to food and to a limited range of organic industrial raw materials. The use of mineral raw materials removed the limit from industrial production in general, both directly by making it possible for an enormous increase in the physical volume of production to take place without prejudice to future supplies of raw materials, and indirectly by demonstrating that the 'powers of nature' were present just as abundantly in the mines as in the land, so that capital invested in industry could yield at least as good a return as investment in the land from the point of view of the community as a whole. There is thus a certain restricted sense in which Malthus has remained more relevant to the modern situation than Adam Smith, for in discussing the limitations imposed upon the growth of population by the size of the supply of food, Malthus was concentrating upon a part of the economy in which it has not been possible as yet to substitute inorganic for organic raw materials. He was mistaken about the rate at which the supply of food could be expanded, but the problem he posed still lives with us today. His argument in a modern setting appears wrong in degree, but right in kind. Adam Smith's discussion of the wealth of nations, on the other hand, appears wrong in the second sense because he was not aware of the new possibilities of increasing production just becoming apparent in his day when the substitution of mineral for vegetable and animal raw materials removed an ancient and important obstacle to industrial growth.

IV

The importance of minerals in general and coal in particular to the development of an industrial economy at the end of the eighteenth century extends beyond the improvement in communications and the possibility of escaping the close limits set to expansion as long as organic raw materials were essential to most industrial processes, for the development of the steam engine is peculiarly a product of the problems of the mining industry.

Although the expansion of mineral production was not subject to the same limitations as the expansion of the production of vegetable and animal materials, the technological problems of increasing production were nevertheless considerable. Perhaps the most intractable was that of draining pits when they were sunk to a depth which made impossible drainage by the cutting of adits to a point on the surface below the level of the seam. Horse gins were useful when the depths were moderate, but at the depths where some of the richest seams of coal and veins of tin and copper occurred a more powerful engine was required if the inflow of water to the workings was to be held in check.[1] The urgent difficulties of the mining industry were the means of turning the Newcomen from an ingenious but unpractical machine into a reliable piece of equipment without which the deeper pits could not have been maintained in production. The early engines of Savery and Newcomen were essentially pumping machines for which the only big market was the mining industry. A few Newcomen engines were used for pumping water from rivers to help with the supply of water to towns, but the majority were used in mines. They were at once essential to the continued expansion in coal production, and virtually unusable without a supply of coal. They are a product of a coal age rather than a wood age and could only be used extensively when mines rather than woodlands were their source of fuel. Otherwise they would have devastated an area of timber as quickly as the early iron industry had done, for the early engines were extremely inefficient and required very large quantities of fuel. Theoretical

---

[1] It has been claimed that three-quarters of the patents issued in England between 1561 and 1668 were connected with the coal industry, either directly, or indirectly, and that a seventh were concerned with the drainage problem. S. F. Mason, *A History of the Sciences* (1953), p. 217.

knowledge of the power of steam had long existed, but the coal industry's problems first provided the catalyst to convert this into workable machinery rather than engaging toys. The first use of steam engines in industries other than mining reflects their background as pumping engines in mines, for they were used initially simply to complete the cycle of water movement from tail-race to mill-pond and so to render water wheels independent of ordinary stream flow and prevent those interruptions to their operation which had previously been inevitable in prolonged dry weather. Watt's improvements to the steam engine (or rather his invention of a steam in place of an atmospheric engine) and his development of methods of gearing which gave rotatory rather than reciprocating motion represent radical improvements upon the earlier Newcomen engines and gave the steam engine great importance in a wide range of industries as time passed. The steam engine more than any other single development, perhaps, made possible the vast increase in individual productivity which was so striking a feature of the Industrial Revolution by providing a source of power which dwarfed human, animal and even hydraulic sources. Yet the machine Watt improved was already widely used in the mining industry, which had fostered its development for several decades.

V

The cotton industry has attracted more attention than any other in discussions of the Industrial Revolution, and since it grew vastly while continuing to use a vegetable raw material, it merits further consideration in the context of this essay. No other major industry grew as quickly as cotton in the late eighteenth century. There was a series of inventions in both spinning and weaving which led to a marked rise in the output per worker. Cotton spinning was the first industrial activity to become organized in factories in the fashion which became normal during the next century. Lancashire became the area which first acquired the full range of features characteristic of the new industrial scene; large urban manufacturing populations living a life divorced from the rhythm of the countryside about them, working in factories, caught up in a web of exchange which connected their livelihood with events throughout the world. Cotton has for long been treated as the *type par excellence* of the new manufacturing industry, the lead-off industry in the take-off into sustained industrial growth.

The cotton industry fits well into the pattern of industrial growth which Adam Smith described. The decisive importance of the size of the market is well illustrated in its history. The attempt to expand production to keep pace with demand caused new mechanical devices to be seized upon eagerly and developed rapidly into reliable manufacturing machinery. There was a steep rise in productivity as workers became more specialized and turned to cotton manufacture as a full-time employment rather than a useful subsidiary source of income. The price of the finished article fell and still further enlarged the market. Once Whitney's gin had proved its worth, the demands of the industry for raw materials could be met by breaking in new land in the southern United States. There was no bottleneck in raw material supply and raw cotton tended to fall rather than rise in price. There is nothing in the story to call in question the assumptions of Adam Smith about the part played by the growth of industry in promoting the wealth of nations. Some coal was used in the preparatory and finishing sections of the industry, but only after a generation of expansion had caused the need for power to outstrip the capabilities of the human arm and the water wheel was the steam engine brought into use, so that the problem of raw material provision was very different in the cotton industry from those industries in which organic raw materials were replaced by inorganic. The example of the cotton industry makes it clear that industrial expansion could go far and fast in some directions without provoking difficulties in raw material supply.

For this very reason, however, the cotton industry, in spite of its importance in the Industrial Revolution, cannot be regarded as a microcosm of the whole process. In particular the great changes in inland transport and in power were not closely connected with the cotton industry. The movement of cotton presented no great difficulties to the methods of goods transport which had been in use for centuries. The movement of raw cotton was measured by the million pound rather than the million ton and bore a far higher value per unit weight than, say, coal. In consequence it was able to support relatively high transport charges without a crippling increase in price. The fact that many early mills were built in quite remote Pennine valleys close to a head of water underlines this point. Similarly, the well-tried sources of industrial power, initially the worker's arms and later the water wheel, sufficed to move the machinery used in the cotton industry during the first two decades of rapid growth at the end of the eighteenth century. The cotton industry benefited substantially from the opening of canal communication between Manchester and Liverpool, both in that the transport charges were lower than by river or on horseback and in that delivery was more reliable and quicker: but the cotton industry did not create a large enough tonnage of traffic to justify the construction of canals. 1800 was the first year in which the import of raw cotton exceeded 50 million pounds in weight, which is only some 23,000 tons, and no more than the annual output of perhaps 150 coal-miners. Even though cotton might produce a much greater revenue per ton-mile than mineral freight it is clear that the cotton industry in itself could offer little inducement to spend capital on the scale necessary to build canals. In so far as the presence of the cotton industry in Lancashire did hasten the construction of canals it was perhaps rather as a consumer of coal and as an employer of labour which consumed coal domestically that it exerted an influence. Again, the cotton industry became an important market for Watt's new engines. Without them it might have lost impetus as the most suitable heads of water were harnessed one by one, leaving only the inaccessible or insufficient to be brought into use. But the history of the development of the steam engine lies outside the cotton industry.

It might indeed even be argued that there is a sense in which the cotton industry was exploiting old lines of development with a new intensity rather than striking out in a radically new direction. There had been periods of technological innovation in the textile industry in the past. When, for example, the spinning wheel superseded the distaff there had been a marked rise in the productivity of the individual spinner. The invention of the knitting machine and the introduction of the Dutch swivel-loom had also in their time brought about important changes in productivity and in the amount of fixed capital per worker. Water power had been used in the fulling of wool and the throwing of silk for centuries. Even the bringing together of many textile workers under one roof was not unknown before the eighteenth century. During the late eighteenth century the cotton industry brought development along old lines to a new pitch of perfection, evolving better machinery in both spinning and weaving and extending the use of water power into spinning. There was a vast increase in the quantity of cotton manufactured. It was produced more cheaply and, after early difficulties with the new machinery had been overcome, the quality of both yarn and cloth was higher than anything achieved in England in the past. In contrast with this the range of industries in which coal replaced wood as the main source of heat might be held to have struck out along a new line of development. The change from organic to inorganic sources of raw material supply led to no sudden or dramatic change in the quantity or quality of production in the industries concerned, yet latent in this change were new possibilities for improvement in the transport of goods and the supply of power to industrial processes. To borrow a biological analogy the raw material bottleneck produced a mutation in raw material supply which proved intensely favourable and led to changes which helped to transform industrial production and ultimately society as a whole.

The temptation to treat the cotton industry as a microcosm of the whole Industrial Revolution has proved difficult to resist. The signs of the new age were first readily apparent in cotton, but its history is not therefore typical of the whole. The fact that the cotton industry was singularly free from raw material supply problems marked it out from many others, at once facilitating its expansion at an early date and isolating it from a range of problems faced and solved by many other industries. Cotton benefited from the new sources of power and better transport facilities, but these were available because of the successful struggle against difficulties of raw material supply which had taken place in other sectors of the economy.

VI

It is natural that special attention should be paid by all those interested in the Industrial Revolution to any aspect of English life which was different from its continental equivalent. Hence the great interest shown in such questions as social mobility and capillarity, the organization of financial affairs and the capital market in England, English agriculture and systems of land tenure, the forms of English government and law, and in exploring any differences between English and Continental demographic patterns. The supply of industrial raw materials may, of course, be treated in the same way. It is not difficult to show that the Continent clung longer to the traditional types of organic industrial raw material, nor is it difficult to suggest reasons for this. Wiebe's price series,[1] for example, suggests that the supply of some types of timber was causing much less difficulty on the Continent than in England in the seventeenth century. Yet it is perhaps more illuminating to dwell on the occasional similarities between England and the Continent than on the general dissimilarity.

The area most like the new English industrial areas was central Belgium. This was the only area on the Continent in which the production of coal in the eighteenth century reached a level at all comparable with that achieved in English coalfields at the same time. Both at Liège and near Charleroi the coal seams outcropped to the surface near the good water communication afforded by the Sambre–Meuse system, and this made possible the development of a wide market for coal at an early date. The Mons coalfield was not so well endowed with natural water communication, but the same problems and opportunities which produced a burst of canal building in England led to a similar development in Mons. The Mons–Condé canal, for

[1] G. Wiebe, *Zur Geschichte der Preisrevolution des XVI. und XVII. Jahrhunderts* (Leipzig, 1895). See esp. Tables 522, 524, and 528.

I

example, was completed in 1814, linking the coalfield area with the industries of Nord. The history of the successful search for coal in the concealed Nord field which resulted in the sinking of the famous mine at Anzin is evidence of how useful even in the middle of the eighteenth century the discovery of coal was judged to be in this part of the Continent. At that time traffic along the valley of the Sambre–Meuse resembled that along the valley of the Severn in England. The metal communes of Maubeuge and Valenciennes, for example, were dependent upon primary iron imported from the *pays de Liège* in the late eighteenth century. Belgian pits were quick to adopt British devices. Already before the turn of the century Belgian pits had reached considerable depths and were using Newcomen engines extensively. Soon after the turn of the century other British developments were absorbed into Belgian practice: the use of the steam engine for winding up coal and men as well as for pumping water, the Davy safety-lamp, and so on. There were independent local contributions to coal-mining and other industrial problems in Belgium at this time. Joseph Chaudron, for example, discovered an improved method of protecting main shafts by using a revetment of iron (the *cuvelage en fer*). Dony succeeded in extracting zinc from calamine. Gas lighting, a Belgian invention,[1] was in use in factories by 1810. The remarkable achievements of the Cockerill family in engineering and textiles at Seraing and Verviers during the first quarter of the nineteenth century form an industrial epic on a scale worthy of comparison with English equivalents of the period. John Cockerill constructed successful coke-fired blast furnaces at Seraing in the 1820s, and built excellent marine steam engines. The advance of central Belgium, in short, was very rapid, and it is perhaps symbolic of this that Neilson's hot blast was widely used there at a time when it was still a novelty in British iron centres outside Scotland.

The history of the rapid acceptance of British industrial advances in the valleys of the Meuse and Sambre is not vastly

---

[1] Minckelers lighted his lecture room with gas in 1785, though it was William Murdoch who in the 1790s showed the commercial possibilities of this method of illumination.

different from the history of their acceptance, say, in the valleys of South Wales. There was, it is true, usually a time lag, though not always longer in the case of Liège than in the case of the less active British areas. In view of the fact that Belgium during the eighteenth and early nineteenth centuries was ruled by other countries and was frequently disturbed by the passage of armies, it is striking how swiftly the areas whose problems and opportunities were similar to those of the new industrial areas of Britain followed the British lead and occasionally improved upon it.

Central Belgium was not unique among Continental industrial areas. The St Etienne region, for example, showed some similar traits, but in the main it is fair to contrast the conservatism of the Continent over industrial raw material supply with the rapid change in England. When Thünen published his book the Ruhr was still an area of agriculture and marshland. The example of central Belgium, however, where change came so rapidly on the heels of developments in similar English areas, stresses in the context of raw material supply two points which are perhaps true of the industrial Revolution as a whole: first that Western Europe was a single economic community within which like circumstances might give rise to similar results; and secondly, that industrial growth was essentially a local rather than a national affair. In this regard it is perhaps unnecessarily inexact to talk of England and the Continent rather than, say, of Lancashire and the valley of the Sambre–Meuse. Each country was made up of a number of regional economies. Within Belgium, for example, the Flemish domestic linen industry was in great straits because of its failure to adopt English methods at just the period of brilliant advance on the Belgian coalfields.

Perhaps the chief advantage in looking at the Industrial Revolution from the standpoint of raw material supply is that it makes it easier to understand the nature of the gap which separates Adam Smith and his world from the world which McCulloch knew. The ordinary categories of economic analysis do not pick up the differences very well. In the world which Adam Smith described there could well exist a technically perfect capitalism, with a developed money market, extensive international trade, many intermediaries between the producer and the ultimate consumer, a divorce between the workers and the ownership of the means of production, and so on. But in this world there was a ceiling to the possible size of industrial production set by the difficulty of expanding raw material supply at constant or declining prices as long as most industrial raw materials were organic. When this was no longer true this ceiling disappeared. Adam Smith's world and that of his Physiocratic predecessors was a world bounded by the fertility of the soil. This was the backcloth to any examination of industrial development. Ninety years later when Jevons published his great work on the coal industry he was prepared to assert firmly that the greatest single factor governing the industrial prospects of any nation must be its wealth in coal.[1] If McCulloch was impatient with Adam Smith it was at least in part because the world in which he lived was different. The weaknesses in his argument would not have escaped Adam Smith if he had the benefit of being able to observe a further half-century of economic history. If he had been privileged to do so, what he would have seen would have convinced him that the use of inorganic raw materials in industry on a vast scale had revealed the existence of 'powers of nature' whose potentialities he had not suspected.

---

[1] 'Coal, in truth, stands not beside but entirely above all other commodities. It is the material energy of the country – the universal aid – the factor in everything we do. With coal almost any feat is possible or easy; without it we are thrown back into the laborious poverty of early times.' W. S. Jevons, *The Coal Question* (London and Cambridge, 1865), p. viii. See also the chapter *Of the Comparative Coal Resources of Different Countries*.

It is interesting to note that Jevons's main concern was that supplies of coal must soon run short in Britain; that mineral raw materials, being exhaustible, were a dangerous basis of national wealth and power.

6 Demand as a Factor in the Industrial Revolution

ELIZABETH WATERMAN GILBOY

[This article was first published in *Facts and Factors in Economic History*, A. H. Cole (ed.) *et al.* (Harvard University Press, 1932).]

I

In the field of economic history as well as that of economic theory there has been a tendency to overemphasize the factor of supply. Precisely as the classical economists were inclined to accept demand as given and constant, most of the economic historians of the nineteenth century concerned themselves with a detailed analysis of changes in the technique of production, the decay and expansion of certain industries, the effects of power machinery upon production, and so on. Little attention has been paid to changes in the nature of demand, even to the undoubted extension of demand, and especially is it true that the mechanism by which these changes occurred has been overlooked. Labour, as well, has been considered rather as a factor in production than as the major portion of the consuming public. When demand has been touched upon at all, it was usually dealt with in vague and general terms, with reference to Adam Smith's theory of the extension of the market. Exceptions occur, of course. Mrs Knowles, Hobson, and a few others were well aware of the significance of developments of the demand factor with respect to the Industrial Revolution. But even they made little attempt to analyse the structure of internal demand; rather they stressed the increase of commerce, and the opening of new markets in undeveloped countries.

Obviously the factory system with its complicated industrial mechanism cannot function profitably without a large and growing demand ready and willing to absorb its products as fast as they are produced. The factory form of organization was not new. It had existed in ancient Rome, again in medieval Florence, and at various times in England and on the Continent, previous to the Industrial Revolution. Before the eighteenth century, however, the factory had never become typical. It existed sporadically to provide a few articles of luxury for the upper classes. The thesis of this essay is, indeed, that the factory could not become typical until demand had been extended and had become sufficiently flexible throughout the entire population to consume the products of large-scale industry. In other words, the Industrial Revolution presupposes a concomitant development and extension of consumption.[1]

The 'extension of the market' school, as those writers who emphasize the phrase of Adam Smith might be called, do not go so far as to examine consumption standards. Why should new countries made accessible to English goods by the expansion of commerce and the greater facilities of transportation have been eager to buy the output of the factories? Why, again, should the home population suddenly afford a market for a greater number of products? These questions have been unanswered for the most part.

Lewinski, for example, explains the origin of the Industrial Revolution in Belgium by the typical 'extension of the market' approach. The growth of the market for Belgian goods was due to the growth of population within the country, primarily, and to the extension of the external market resulting from political alliances, first with France and later with Holland.[2] He places emphasis upon the increase in population as indicating an increase in demand which forced industry to adopt new production methods, largely because of the action of diminishing returns.[3] It is difficult to see why an increase of population as

---

[1] I am greatly indebted to Professor Gay for pointing out to me the importance of the analysis of consumption in connexion with the Industrial Revolution. He is, in fact, the only person known to me who has stated the above hypothesis definitely and clearly, though not in print. I owe him the impetus which started me upon the investigation of demand, not only in connexion with the Industrial Revolution, but in general.

[2] *L'Evolution Industrielle de la Belgique* (1911).　　　[3] Ibid., p. 58.

such should necessarily lead to an increase in demand. The result might just as plausibly be a decrease in the standard of living of the population. The pressure of population upon subsistence, reducing the standard of living of the majority of the population to a bare minimum of existence, is a doctrine which has been familiarized by Malthus and Ricardo. And it has been a fact in the case of China, and, until recently, of India. If population increase were in itself a sufficient reason for increasing demand, calling forth more highly developed methods of production, the Industrial Revolution ought to be in an advanced stage in both India and China. Increase in population cannot by itself increase demand except in the case of a people with a standard of living so firmly intrenched that any lowering of the standard is implacably resisted. Then the increase in numbers may well serve as a stimulus to the discovery of profitable means of improving the technique of production. Undoubtedly this is what occurred in Belgium, although it is not brought out by Lewinski. Even when population increase does increase demand, it is not usually the most important aspect of the change in demand and probably would not alone lead to extensive industrial reorganization. An expansion of the standard of living of the population, as well as the growth of new wants, is necessary.

Mrs Knowles and the Hammonds seem to have had some such process in mind when they selected commerce as the cause of the Industrial Revolution in England.[1] They point to the new commodities introduced into general consumption as a result of seventeenth- and eighteenth-century commerce, and admit that an increase in the general demand of the population took place at the same time. The process by which this widespread increase in demand occurred, however, is not analysed; and it may be pointed out in passing that the Hammonds' implicit admission of a rise in the standard of living of the population as a whole in eighteenth-century England is somewhat inconsistent with their theory of increasing misery of the working classes after 1750.

[1] L. Knowles, *The Industrial and Commercial Revolutions in Great Britain . . .* (1924); T. and B. Hammond, *The Rise of Modern Capitalism* (1925).

An unusual emphasis upon the significance of demand is to be found in Hobson's *Evolution of Modern Capitalism*. His fourth essential condition for the development of capitalism is 'the existence of large, accessible markets *with populations willing and economically able to consume the products of capitalist industry*'.[1] If these markets do not have populations willing and able to consume industrial products on a large scale, the type of business made widespread by the Industrial Revolution cannot exist. Hobson is aware of this and also makes consumption an integral part of his theory of over-saving as the cause of business cycles. That theory cannot be examined here, but it is of some interest to note Hobson's stress upon the part played by demand. It is made apparent again in his treatment of wages, in which he examines the justification of high wages from the point of view of the consumption of the workers and of the community as a whole.

Pillai comes very near to the point of view of the present paper in the initial pages of his study of the Industrial Revolution in India. He contends that the extremely slow penetration of modern industrialism into India is due to the difficulties of changing the standards of consumption of the general population.[2] Probably there are still other authors besides those mentioned here who have recognized the significance of demand. None of them, however, pay any attention to the process by which demand changes. Hobson comes nearest to analysing the mechanism by which changes in demand occur, but even he deals with the term in a rather vague way and links his analysis to an idealistic scheme of social progress.

It is therefore the task of the present essay, in so far as it can be done within the limits of a brief paper, to sketch the relation between changes in demand and changes in the technique of production. The theoretical argument will be illustrated principally, but not entirely, by the situation in England in the eighteenth century, at the time when the radical industrial changes which are classed under the heading of the Industrial Revolution were taking place.

[1] See p. 2.   [2] *Economic Conditions in India* (1925).

II

The theory is simple. It may be briefly stated thus: necessary concomitants of the growth of large-scale production, and especially of its initial stages, are (1) changes in the shape of the demand schedule, to use Marshallian terminology,[1] or in the nature of demand, of the various layers of consumption within the general population; (2) a shift in the demand schedules of the group, or an increase in demand; (3) the introduction of new wants; and (4) mobility of individuals within and between the various classes of the population. In other words, the tastes of the population are changed both in nature and in quantity, new commodities are incorporated into the consumption of the group, and there is considerable shifting between the members of the various groups within the community. If any one of these factors is present, the others are likely to emerge. They are all interrelated. They mark a society which is socially unstable, in which standards of living are changing, and in which class lines are not clearly drawn.

A society in which the standards of consumption of a majority of the population are fixed and stable, wherein people are contented with what they have and desire nothing more, scarcely provides fertile soil for the sowing of industrial changes. Even an increase in population may have little effect in stimulating methods of production. If diminishing returns set in, the excess population may emigrate or die of starvation or plague, or war may ensue. New production methods *may* be invented, especially with a net population increase, but as a rule a complete overturn of the social structure is needed as well. The continued social stability of medieval life is a case in point; then the standard of living of each class was fixed by

[1] For the benefit of the general reader not versed in Marshallian economics, it may be explained that 'demand schedule' is the term for a hypothetical list of prices and quantities, expressing the relation between the number of units of a commodity which an individual or a group *would* buy and the price per unit, at any one time under given conditions. Mathematically, price is usually expressed as a variable function of quantity. The standard of living of a person or group may be looked upon as composed of a series of interrelated schedules of this sort, all of which may change in shape and position, affecting other schedules in so doing.

custom and tradition, and centuries elapsed before this stability could be broken down.

In order that a shift in the demand schedule may occur, individuals must be able to buy more units of a commodity at the same price, or the same amount of the commodity at a higher price. In other words, the entire schedule must shift upwards, indicating a greater buying power. There must therefore be an increase in the real income of the population. Real wages must rise, either through a decrease in prices or through a rise in money income, so that the majority of the population have more to spend.

The spread of new wants throughout the majority of the population is one of the most active forces leading to changes in standards of consumption. The introduction of new commodities leads people possessed of an economic surplus to try this and that, and finally to include many new articles in their customary standard of life.[1] If the economic surplus is not at hand, supposed necessaries may be neglected in order to obtain novelties, or individuals may be motivated to work harder in order to obtain the economic surplus. The mechanism by which these new wants are incorporated into all classes involves interclass competition, not only in consumption but in production: there must be sufficient mobility within the groups so that some individuals, at least, actually move from one group to another, while many more are actuated by a belief that they can do so.

The process is something like this. New articles are made available by commerce and taken up as a fashion by the wealthy and leisured members of society. The process may end there. If the various classes are not sufficiently closely related so that interclass competition in consumption is possible, if the general population have neither the desire nor the means to experiment with these new commodities, they will end as they began, articles of luxury for the rich. Commerce in the Middle Ages was largely in such luxuries; it was not until the seventeenth

[1] See Hazel Kyrk, *Theory of Consumption*, for a statement of the existence of an economic surplus, and an available supply of varied economic goods as a stimulus to consumption change.

and eighteenth centuries that the ordinary individual would or could begin to include such goods in his own consumption. It did not occur to the average villein or serf to desire spices or jewels or silken robes. He expected to live and die in his own stratum, content with a simple diet and coarse and unornamented clothing. Envy of the upper classes, closely followed by an attempt to imitate them, what Defoe called 'apeing one's betters', is a comparatively modern phenomenon. The removal of political, legal, and economic restrictions upon the lower classes, the breakdown of feudal and manorial customs, were essential to its development.

As Tawney observes:

> The tendency and direction of the forces released by the Industrial Revolution, if that phrase is still to be retained, are not open to question. They were those described by Sir Henry Maine, when he wrote of 'the beneficent private war which makes one man strive to climb on the shoulders of another and remain there'. Compared with that of most earlier periods, the economic system which it created was fluid and elastic.[1]

The fluid and elastic system was not entirely created by the Industrial Revolution. It existed prior to the development of the Industrial Revolution – or such a great economic change could not have happened when and where it did – and was then enhanced in turn by the industrial development.

It is part of Tawney's criticism of the modern economic and social order to deplore 'that beneficent struggle'. He would substitute social and collective goals for those of individual gain in wealth and power. It is extremely dubious whether modern industrial society could have begun or could continue without the type of individualistic competition which he most decries. It may be limited and controlled, the rules of the game may be made more stringent and applicable to all, but it must be there. Ethically it may be undesirable; but economically it is essential to the development of modern industry.

Once society is sufficiently mobile, the luxury articles of the

[1] R. H. Tawney, *Equality* (1930), p. 39.

rich will seep down through the different social ranks, and perhaps end by becoming a necessity for all. By this time the upper classes will have taken up some other article of fashion. A contemporary described the process well:

> In England the several ranks of men slide into each other almost imperceptibly; and a spirit of equality runs through every part of the constitution. Hence arises a strong emulation in all the several stations and conditions to vie with each other; and a perpetual restless ambition in each of the inferior ranks to raise themselves to the level of those immediately above them. In such a state as this fashion must have an uncontrolled sway. And a fashionable luxury must spread through it like a contagion.[1]

Although this sort of thing occurred prior to the eighteenth century, it did not take place in a sufficiently general fashion to cause widespread comment. But at that time, eighteenth-century pamphleteers in England burst forth into a lamentation upon luxury in general and particularly the luxury of the lower classes. More will be said about this later.

Still another aspect of the problem exists which is not without interest. The qualitative and quantitative changes in demand noted above may serve as a stimulus to production in another way. So far we have only mentioned the fact that demand must increase and change in order to absorb the output of industry. It may also be true that changing consumption standards will act as an impetus to labour on the side of production. A transition has to be made from labour which is independent and which works in its own home, at its own time, to labour which works under strict discipline in a factory. Usually it is assumed that labour was forced by circumstances to make this change. Certainly it is true that in England, at any rate, the acceleration of the enclosure movement, dispossessing agricultural labour in many districts, occurred conveniently about the time when masses of unskilled labour were needed in the new factories. It is true, as well, that the state disposed of

[1] [T. Forster], *An Enquiry into the Causes of the Present High Price of Provisions* (London, 1767), p. 41.

paupers by transferring them by the cartload from parish work-houses to factories.[1] What could labour do but submit?

On the other hand, many labourers may have been motivated by the desire for increased consumption of material goods, whetted by the taste for luxury already acquired. They may have been willing to submit to the routine and dependent regime of the factory because wages there were higher and steadier. There is reason to think that this was true in the north of England, at least. Redford sees in this fact one explanation of the steady and wave-like migration of labour from the countryside to the town. He goes so far as to state that the difference in standard of living, which was in favour of the industrial town, was a motivating force in impelling labour to the industrial centres.[2]

Changes in demand or consumption, therefore, may be looked upon not only as necessary adjuncts to industrial change in the sense of providing a continually expanding and varying market, but as stimuli on the production side, too. As Malthus put it:

> It is not the most pleasant employment to spend eight hours a day in a counting house. Nor will it be submitted to after the common necessaries and conveniences of life are obtained, unless adequate motives are presented to the mind of the man of business. Among these motives is undoubtedly the desire of advancing his rank, and contending with the landlord in the enjoyment of leisure, as well as of foreign and domestic luxuries.[3]

Miss Kyrk stated the same idea more universally when she said, 'For the sake of gains as consumers, individuals consent to more hazardous and less interesting work as workers.'[4] In India the inverse has been found to be true; that is, when labourers have satisfied their fairly simple wants, which can be done in three or four days' work a week, they do not appear

[1] See Unwin, *Samuel Oldknow and the Arkwrights* (1924). Also cf. W. E. Rappard, *La Revolution industrielle . . . en Suisse* (1914), p. 231. The factory workers of the printed-cloth industry were recruited from the poorest elements in the population.

[2] A. Redford, *Labour Migration in England* (1924), p. 60.

[3] *Principles of Political Economy* (2nd edn, 1835), p. 403.   [4] *Op. cit.*, p. 65.

at the factory.[1] What is to make them continue labour which is disagreeable to them, if their material wants are satisfied? As may be imagined, the establishment of the factory system in India has been attended with many difficulties.

Of course, there have always been those who argued that necessity was the only spur to industry and efficiency. This view was particularly popular among the eighteenth-century English mercantilists whose aim was to keep labour cost, in the sense of wages, as low as possible in order that England might outsell competitors in world markets. Sir William Temple expressed their views perfectly when he said that 'the only way to make them [the labourers] temperate and industrious, is to lay them under the necessity of labouring all the time they can spare from meals and sleep, in order to procure the necessaries of life'.[2] Quotations of this sort could be multiplied without end. The question of necessity versus luxury as a motivating force to increase the efficiency of labour and the product of industry engendered a hot philosophical controversy between the mercantilists and their opponents. In more recent times the theory opposite to that of mercantilism has become more popular. The economy of high wages is a doctrine of which one hears a good deal.

Theoretically, then, it is possible to conclude that far-reaching and widespread industrial changes cannot occur except in a society in which demand and consumption standards are undergoing swift and radical readjustment. Such a society is characterized by mobility between classes, the introduction of new commodities leading to the development of new wants, and a rise in real income of the people as a whole. Let us examine briefly the origin of the Industrial Revolution in the light of these ideas.

III

The social and economic milieu of eighteenth-century England formed the background for the first appearance of the Industrial

---

[1] Pillai, op. cit., Chapter IX.
[2] *A Vindication of Commerce and the Arts* (London, 1786), p. 534.

Revolution. From a country predominantly rural, with the greater part of industry carried on in the homes of the workers under various forms of the putting-out system, it was transformed by the end of the century into a country of growing industrialism with factories supplanting the home as the producing unit. It is unnecessary to describe the nature and process of this industrial change. It has been done by many economic historians and by no one more competently than by Mantoux. It may at least be hazarded, although the data are scarce and contradictory, that the standard of living of the general population was increasing at the same time.

The available wage data indicate that the wages of common day labour were certainly increasing in the districts most closely connected with economic expansion.[1] In the north of England (the wage material is for the North and West Ridings of Yorkshire, and Lancashire) the money wages of unskilled labour had risen from a median of 9*d*. per day in 1700 to 1*s*. 9*d*. per day by 1790. During the same period the journeyman's daily wage had gone up from 1*s*. to 2*s*. 3*d*. The rise was especially rapid after 1760. Within ten years the labourer's rate went from 1*s*. to 1*s*. 6*d*., the journeyman's from 1*s*. 6*d*. to 2*s*.; whereas it had taken the first fifty years of the century for the rates to go from 9*d*. to 1*s*. and from 1*s*. to 1*s*. 6*d*., respectively. This upward swing of wages appeared as characteristically in the agricultural districts of the North Riding as in the industrial sections of Lancashire and the West Riding. Real wages, as measured in terms of the labourers' most important article of diet, oat bread, appear to have risen, too, by the end of the century. Other evidence as to the living conditions of the labouring classes gleaned from local records and descriptions of labouring life show a real improvement towards the end of the century, at least for the class of labour under discussion.[2]

[1] E. W. Gilboy, 'Wages in Eighteenth Century England', *Journal of Economic and Business History*, Vol. II, No. 4 (August 1930), pp. 603-29. The statistical material for the analysis of wages and prices summarized above is given in more detail in this paper.

[2] See A. P. Wadsworth and J. de L. Mann, *The Cotton Trade and Industrial Lancashire 1600-1780* (1931), Bk. IV. Mr Wadsworth's evidence as to the condition of the workers in the cotton industry, especially of the weavers, is conflicting.

The balance of contemporary observation points in that direction.

A similar rise in real wages took place in London and the metropolitan district surrounding it. The rise is not as consistent nor as great as in the northern districts, but the median daily rate for the common labourer increased from 1s. 7d. in 1700 to 2s. in 1787. At the same period the wages of craftsmen went from 2s. 6d. to 3s. 2d. Most of this rise occurred before 1750. Wheat prices – again measuring by the chief food item of the labourers' budget – were falling slightly during the first part of the century, and rising during the second half. Subsidiary evidence as to the food, clothing, and general living conditions of the workers provide grounds for assuming a net gain in consumption by the end of the century. The same conclusion, it may be noted, was reached by Mrs George, purely on the basis of pamphlet and general descriptive material.[1]

The data for the west of England are the least satisfactory of the sections investigated. There is no foundation, at any rate, for a conclusion as to rising consumption standards in this district. The median daily wage rate of common labour fluctuated in Gloucestershire around 1s. from 1736 to 1787, the only period for which figures were obtained. Craftsmen's wages were approximately 1s. 6d. per day for most of the period. Barley prices, representing the principal diet of the labourers, showed, if anything, a slight trend upwards, with extraordinarily high prices in the years of bad harvests, which appear to have afflicted the west with especial distress. Food riots were

---

There are no comparable wage figures for various parts of the century. Arthur Young's figures for 1769 indicate that some of the wages were even lower than day-labouring rates, although the check weavers' were somewhat higher. The formation of the early weavers' societies, and their activities in trying to raise wages and improve working conditions, were the result of recurring periods of want due to bad harvests, wars, etc. Mr Wadsworth's material leans towards the depressing side, although he cites some data as to the increase of luxury among the working population. He does not commit himself, however, on the course of the standard of living of the weavers during the century. Probably the question must be left open until wages are specifically investigated.

[1] M. D. George, *London Life in the Eighteenth Century* (1924).

prevalent all over the country in the fifties and sixties, but struck the western counties with particular force.[1]

The apparent stability or, possibly, decline in the standard of living of the Gloucestershire labourer is of interest in connexion with a suggestion noted in the previous section. The decay of the woollen industry of the west during the eighteenth century is well known. It was supplanted by the rising textile industry of the north. The introduction of the factory system occasioned riots against machines wherever they were introduced. In the north these uprisings against the mechanism of modern industry eventually subsided. In the west, however, the workers refused to use the new machines and continued to oppose their introduction. Possibly there is a connexion between the continued opposition of labour to machinery, the decline of the woollen industry of the west, and the low and unchanging standard of living characteristic of the working classes. It might be suggested that the impetus of a changing material standard was lacking, and consequently labouring-class opposition to mechanized labour in a factory could not be overcome. At least, it is plausible to suggest that this may have been a contributing factor to the decay of the industry, which depended, of course, on many other factors as well.

It is unwise to generalize about England as a whole. Distinct regional differences in the real and money wages of common labour in at least three sections of the country have been found. There may be other regional divergences; the study of wages in other trades may tell a different story. Contemporary literature, however, indicates that the situation of London and the north was more typical of the country than that of the west. Eighteenth-century social and political pamphlets are full of allusions to the growth of luxury among the lower classes. Some wrote to deplore it, others to praise it, but most writers noted its existence. Even those who stressed the darker side of working-class life were likely to let slip observations upon the inclusion of tea, wheat bread, sugar, and other luxuries of the day in the labourer's diet. On the basis of this pamphlet material alone, Lecky, an astute and eminent historian,

[1] See Arthur Young, *Tour to the Southern Counties* (1772), p. 340.

K

concluded that the standard of living of the general population had risen during the century.[1] The amount of contemporary comment upon the growth of luxury is so great that it cannot be entirely ignored by the least optimistic of investigators. Some basis of fact must have existed.

It is clear that tea, sugar, and wheat bread became incorporated into the general working-class diet during the century. Meat was eaten more frequently. Cotton and silk clothes were worn by the poor as well as by the rich. More money was spent on recreation, in the form of frequenting fairs, interludes, etc.[2] Conditions in some of the new industrial towns offered better and more sanitary living conditions for the average worker than had been known before.[3] We may conclude tentatively that the consumption of the average labourer was more varied, and greater in amount by the end of the century than at the beginning.

The evidence on interclass mobility and competition is fully as difficult to evaluate. Instances occur in which labourers rose to become managers and even owners of factories. Redford quotes examples of apprentices rising to the position of manager of a mill, and the Reverend William MacRitchie, a contemporary observer, writing of opportunities for advancement in the Sheffield cutlery works, comments, doubtless with exaggeration, on 'people rising every day from nothing to eminence, by dint of industry'.[4] Wadsworth remarks of Lancashire: 'In contrast with the regulated industry of France, or with the sixteenth century ideal of an ordered distributive state in which each class performed its appropriate functions,

---

[1] *History of England in the Eighteenth Century* (1883), Vol. VI, p. 186: 'These complaints of growing extravagance in the industrial classes were too common in the latter half of the eighteenth century not to rest on some real foundation.'

[2] Cf. George, Botsford, and many others. Evidence as to the popularity of amusements comes from Quarter Sessions Records, which record the efforts of the Justices of the Peace to decrease the number of these entertainments as injurious to the morals of the lower classes. Middlesex County Records are full of such indictments.

[3] Cf. the description of Mellor in Unwin, op. cit.; also Redford, op. cit., p. 30.

[4] *Diary of a Tour through Great Britain in 1795* (1897), p. 67.

this Manchester society possessed variety and spontaneity. But it appears almost rigid and bound by custom in comparison with working class life half a century later. . . .'[1] His own evidence throws little light on the rise of the weaver from a small master to a manufacturer. The later eighteenth century, however, appears to have been one of those periods in which the growth of new enterprise, taking place at an unusually rapid rate, so upset the customary equilibrium of social and economic arrangements that individuals were able to transcend class barriers.

Contemporaries expostulated upon competition in consumption between classes. It was complained that servants could not be told from their mistresses; that class distinction was disappearing from the countryside; and that the lower classes no longer knew their position in life.[2] For instance, Davis remarked that 'a fondness for Dress may be said to be the folly of the age, and it is to be lamented, that it has nearly destroyed those becoming marks whereby the several classes of society were formerly distinguished'.[3] The phenomenon was especially noticed in urban districts, in London more than anywhere else, where servants provided the link between the habits of consumption of the upper and lower classes. Down through each rank in the social scale conspicuous consumption of all kinds was imitated. Fielding describes the process as follows: 'Thus while the Nobleman will emulate the Grandeur of a Prince the Gentleman will aspire to the proper state of the Nobleman, the Tradesman steps from behind his Counter into the vacant Place of the Gentleman. . . .'[4]

It cannot be doubted in general that eighteenth-century England exhibited signs of social instability. How inclusive as to region and class of worker the increase of standard of living, how extensive the interclass competition in consumption and production, and how great the luxury of the labourers all remain to be investigated more thoroughly. The undoubted

[1] Op. cit., p. 325.
[2] For example, Defoe, *Giving Alms No Charity* (1704); the *Great Law of Subordination* (1724).
[3] *Friendly Advice to Industrious and Frugal Persons* (1817), p. 23.
[4] *Enquiry into . . . Increase of Robbers* (1753), p. 4.

distress of certain periods, certain sections, and certain classes of workers cannot be disregarded. The fate of the hand-loom weavers, in both England and Switzerland, is a depressing tale. Nor can the evils of the early factories be overlooked. On the other hand, these unfavourable elements must not be over-emphasized as they frequently have been in the past. For the present, it may be assumed that the balance was in favour of an increase of the standard of living.

The initiation of the Industrial Revolution in other countries appears to have been marked with some of the same characteristics. The Swiss weavers were very prosperous in the eighteenth century and formed the basis for the political agitation of the early 1800s. Rappard quotes a contemporary to the effect that 'it was relatively easy to rise from the rank of manual worker to that of head of the industry'.[1] In contrast, he is inclined to stress the misery of the early factories after the manner of the Hammonds. Children and beggars were the labouring force of many of the first factories, in degrading conditions. In this case, why did migration occur from the country to the cities, if the result were only misery? Figures are given to show that factories were supplied with very little labour from the home district. Visitors, too, commented favourably on the living conditions of the Swiss working classes, despite a lower level of wages than in other countries. Rappard attributes this to foreign optimism and apparently disregards the fact that the standard of living may have risen. Still, he cites contemporaries on the instability and discontent of the early factory workers, their ambition for material well-being, and their going from factory to factory in search of better conditions. These conditions are not dissimilar to those which we have seen to characterize eighteenth-century England.

Pillai attributes the slow development of the factory system in India in large part to the low standard of living of the workers, and their strict caste organization which makes competition between classes unthinkable. He gives some evidence – not very complete – of a rise in wages of the lowest class of workers and of the breakdown of the caste system coincident

[1] Op. cit., p. 242.

with the growth of the factory system. The willingness of workers to labour more steadily, in the hope of acquiring the articles of comfort and luxury creeping in through the influence of foreigners, appears to be increasing.[1]

The United States imported the Industrial Revolution in a late stage and developed industrially in an exceptionally short period. It may be observed briefly that American society has been noted since its origin for its lack of class distinction, and for mobility between the indistinct class groups which did grow up; and for its general restlessness and striving for material comfort. America, in fact, exhibited in an intensified form the conditions out of which the Industrial Revolution grew in England.

In conclusion, we may say that demand is an important factor in facilitating the occurrence of industrial change, on the basis of *a priori* reasoning. The importance of stimulating demand is, indeed, extensively recognized by modern producers. Whereas in the early stages of the Industrial Revolution demand was, if anything, in the van of production, today the reverse is true. Over-expanded industries resort to high-pressure salesmanship of the most farfetched nature in order to increase a demand already existent, or to arouse it where there is none.

The continued investigation of demand in relation to the Industrial Revolution is to be urged. Elaborate statistical researches cannot be expected. It would certainly be impossible to concoct even the most dubious 'statistical' demand curve from eighteenth-century data. It is possible, however, to obtain data on wages and the prices of the main foodstuffs and to indicate crudely the course of real wages. Contemporary comment may be compared and sifted in order to obtain a net balance of opinion. The use of eighteenth-century English sources has led to the conclusion that changes in demand played an important part in the initiation of the Industrial Revolution. Changing consumption standards, the increase of population and shifting of individuals from class to class, and a

[1] Op. cit., p. 135.

rise in real income provided a stimulus to the expansion of industry which must not be underestimated. Although the mistake must not be made of exaggerating, in turn, the influence of demand, its significant relation to changes in production should be clearly recognized.

7 England and France in the Eighteenth Century: A Comparative Analysis of Two Economic Growths

F. CROUZET

[This article is edited from *Angleterre et France au XVIIIe Siècle. Essai d'Analyse Comparée de Deux Croissances Economiques*, first published in *Annales*, *21*, 2, 1966. Translated by Mrs J. Sondheimer.]

The economic historian interested in the key problem of growth is bound to find the comparative approach particularly fruitful. A systematic comparison of the eighteenth-century English economy with that of another country – and France as the leading Continental power at that time seems the obvious choice – should bring out more clearly what factors were peculiar to England and might therefore have determined what is a unique phenomenon, the English Industrial Revolution of the eighteenth century.

The first point to be made is that the forwardness of England and the backwardness of France, clearly noticeable on the eve of the French Revolution, were not of sudden or recent appearance; this disparity between the two countries had already been evident early in the century, say at the death of Louis XIV. Moreover, to find an explanation for the contrasts between the social and economic structures of France and England we should have to look at the problem over a long period (going well back into the Middle Ages).[1] That task

[1] One would stress, for example, the importance of wool in English history: wool production, the wool trade and woollen manufacture early made England part of the international economy and stimulated the rise of capitalism.

cannot be attempted here, but it must at least be stressed that developments during the seventeenth century had a different effect on the two economies, which partly accounts for the time-lag between them at the beginning of the eighteenth century.

As is well known, a similar point was made some thirty years ago by J. U. Nef, who pressed it very hard with his assertion that the reason why England was the first country to undergo the eighteenth-century Industrial Revolution was simply that, unlike other countries and particularly France, she had already undergone a first industrial revolution in the late sixteenth and early seventeenth centuries, which meant that her lead had been established some two centuries earlier than was generally thought.[1] But this thesis has been strongly criticized from the British side, and little of it remains intact today.[2] The 'first English industrial revolution' existed chiefly in Nef's imagination: he attached far too much importance to a few technical innovations, to the understandably fast growth of a handful of new industries (coal excepted, their role was a very minor one – yet he ignored the slow growth in the major woollen industry), and lastly to a few non-representative cases of entrepreneurial giantism.[3]

[1] J. U. Nef, 'A comparison of industrial growth in France and England from 1540 to 1640', *Journal of Political Economy*, XLIV (1936), pp. 289–317, 505–33, 643–66; see also by the same author: 'The progress of technology and the growth of large-scale industry in Great Britain, 1540–1640', *The Economic History Review*, v (1934), pp. 3–24; 'Prices and industrial capitalism in France and England, 1540–1640', ibid., VII (1937), pp. 155–85; 'L'industrie et l'État en France et en Angleterre (1540–1640)', *Revue Historique*, CXCI (1941), pp. 21–53, 193–231.

[2] See particularly D. C. Coleman, 'Industrial growth and industrial revolutions', *Economica*, n.s. XXIII (1956), reprinted in E. M. Carus-Wilson (ed.), *Essays in Economic History*, III (London, 1962), pp. 345–7; D. C. Coleman, 'Technology and economic history, 1500–1750', *The Economic History Review*, 2nd series, XI (1959), pp. 506–7, 509–10, 512; B. E. Supple, *Commercial crisis and change in England, 1600–1642* (Cambridge, 1959), pp. 2–8; F. J. Fisher (ed.), *Essays in the economic and social history of Tudor and Stuart England in honour of R. H. Tawney* (Cambridge, 1961), pp. 6–7; Y. S. Brenner, 'The inflation of prices in England, 1551–1650', *The Economic History Review*, 2nd series, XV (1962), pp. 271–3.

[3] On the other hand, Nef overstated the stagnation of French industry during the same period, in that he ignored the textile industries on the French side of the channel, above all linen and wool. He also went much too far when he spoke of a 'phenomenal acceleration' in English industrial output between 1540 and 1640.

Nevertheless, Nef deserves our thanks for having stressed the importance of the fast rise in English coal production and consumption during the century after 1540, and its influence on technological progress through stimulating the development and adoption of some completely new techniques, such as furnaces fired by coal or coke, which were quite unknown on the Continent. This early adoption of mineral fuels gave English inventiveness an impetus which proved to be lasting and which in France was lacking.[1] Again, it seems that Nef was right in maintaining that between 1540 and 1640 England had an absolute lead over France in mining and metal production and also had a higher output per head for products such as woollen goods and glass, and possibly for industrial output as a whole.[2]

However, it was after 1640 rather than before that significant disparities between the economic evolution of the two countries appeared. As is well known, recent research has produced a black picture of French economic history in the 'tragic seventeenth century'. This work has shown that after a relatively prosperous start to the century, the 1630s saw the beginning of a long period of stagnation and decline – turning in mid-century during the Fronde into collapse – which lasted up to the 1720s. Prices – and especially food prices – over the century show a downward trend, and more significantly, extreme instability; there were frequent and violent economic and demographic crises, attended by terrible mortalities; there was monetary famine and 'tightness of money', which crippled business activity and brought down rents and industrial and commercial profits; there was unemployment and pauperism. In view of all this, it is no wonder that industrial production stagnated and even declined.[3] Colbert's policy of industrialization

[1] W. H. Chaloner and A. E. Musson, *Industry and Technology* (London, 1963, *A Visual History of Modern Britain*), pp. 20-1, 24-5, 29; 'The origins of the Industrial Revolution', *Past and Present*, XVII (1960), p. 76 (report of a colloquium on this subject).

[2] J. U. Nef, 'A comparison . . .', op. cit., p. 663.

[3] See P. Goubert, *Beauvais et le Beauvaisis de 1600 à 1730. Contribution à l'histoire sociale de la France du XVIIe siècle* (Paris, 1960), pp. 585-91, 595-6; graphs, 126-30, pp. 116-19 of the supplement; P. Deyon, 'Variations de la production textile aux XVIe et XVIIe siècles: Sources et premiers résultats', *Annales E.S.C.*, XVIII (1963),

was really nothing but a desperate effort to counteract this declining trend; it was undertaken in the highly unfavourable conditions of deflation, falling prices, incomes, and consumption, and ended in semi-failure.[1] Although some of his new industrial undertakings survived and developed later, many others declined and quickly disappeared; and on the whole, if there was any increase in total industrial output under Colbert's government, which is not certain, it was not very pronounced. It is true that recent research has shown that despite two great wars, several famines and protestant emigration, there were signs of recovery in the French economy during the latter part of the reign of Louis XIV, long thought to have been catastrophic. This may well reveal a rising underlying trend, a sign heralding the post-1715 growth, but any such recovery was largely counteracted by the bad effects of wars and famines.[2] Therefore, even if there are a few positive items to enter on the French balance sheet for the seventeenth century, the general picture remains most unfavourable, and nowadays it is accepted that the population of France in 1715 and 1720 was lower than it had been in 1640.[3]

On the English side of the Channel the picture is certainly different, and English historians are on the whole moderately optimistic in their estimation of England's economic performance during the seventeenth century. England was not, of course, totally unaffected by the adverse economic climate of the seventeenth century; there were periods of difficulty and stagnation, for example in the 1620s, during the Civil War and at moments in the wars against Louis XIV; England's main

---

pp. 947, 950–3. Also R. Baehrel, *Une croissance: La Basse-Provence rurale (fin du XVIe siècle, 1789). Essai d'économie historique statistique* (Paris, 1961).

[1] See Goubert's pessimistic estimate of the results of Colbert's policy at Beauvais, op. cit., pp. 584, 596–7; also pp. 619, 621–4.

[2] P. Léon, 'La crise de l'économie française à la fin du règne de Louis XIV (1685–1715)', *Information historique*, XVIII (1956), pp. 132–7; P. Deyon, op. cit., pp. 953–5. P. Goubert, in his *Louis XIV et vingt millions de Français* (Paris, 1966) and *L'avènement du Roi-soleil 1661* (Paris, 1967), has somewhat revised his pessimistic picture of the seventeenth-century French economy.

[3] P. Goubert, op. cit., p. 622; E. Labrousse, *Le paysan français des Physiocrates à nos jours* (Paris, Cours de Sorbonne, 1962), p. 13.

industry, woollen manufacture, went through a series of crises and its growth over the century as a whole was relatively modest; chronic poverty and underemployment were serious problems.[1] But there is nothing to compare with the recurrent violent crises or the deep and lasting depression to be seen in France after 1630. The reversal in the trend of price movements and of the economy in general reached England later than France, about 1650, and in England the subsequent fall in prices was smaller, while short-term price fluctuations seem to have been less violent, less irregular, and hence less injurious to economic activity.[2] F. J. Fisher was able to conclude that the global output of agriculture and industry increased slowly but appreciably during the century, and that despite the rise in population, average income per head probably rose.[3]

There are also other signs of economic progress, especially after 1660, for which there is no parallel in France: for example, the expansion of the English home market, due principally to the growth of London, which far exceeded that of Paris; the 'frontier-like' development of the northern and western counties;[4] and the fast and prolonged growth during the seventeenth century of English foreign trade, largely thanks to early colonial expansion, which meant that from the 1660s England had an important trade in the re-export of exotic products, a trade which continued to rise and was the chief factor in the

[1] See on this point the important article by D. C. Coleman, 'Labour in the English economy of the seventeenth century', *The Economic History Review*, 2nd series, VIII (1956), pp. 280–95.

[2] J. Meuvret, 'La géographie des prix des céréales et les anciennes économies européennes: prix méditerranéens, prix continentaux, prix atlantiques à la fin du XVIIᵉ siècle', *Revista da Economia*, no. 2 (1951), p. 69; P. Chaunu, 'Le renversement de la tendance majeure des prix et des activités au XVIIᵉ siècle. Problèmes de fait et de méthode', *Studi in onore di Amintore Fanfani*, IV, pp. 238–40, 251–2; Y. S. Brenner, op. cit., pp. 276, 281–2; G. N. Clark, *The Wealth of England from 1496 to 1760* (London, 1946), pp. 108–10; E. H. Phelps Brown and S. V. Hopkins, 'Seven centuries of the prices of consumables, compared with builders' wage-rates', *Economica*, n.s., XXIII (1956), pp. 299–301, 305, 312–13.

[3] F. J. Fisher, *Essays . . .*, op. cit., p. 3; F. J. Fisher, 'The sixteenth and seventeenth centuries. The Dark Ages in English economic history?', *Economica*, n.s., XXIV (1957), pp. 6–9, 12, 15, 16.

[4] F. J. Fisher, in *Economica*, pp. 10–11.

growth of English trade as a whole, at a time when French colonies and colonial trade were still relatively insignificant.[1]

Thanks to this slow but quite steady growth, at the beginning of the eighteenth century England already had a definite lead over France in several important fields.[2] First, in agriculture: various technical improvements were now in use over a large part of the country, productivity was higher and more regular than in France, a fact which, together with England's geographical advantages, helps to explain why bad crops were less disastrous in their effects. Secondly, in industrial technology: the earlier innovations which resulted from the use of coal as a fuel had been supplemented by the great burst of inventive activity of the late seventeenth and early eighteenth centuries, which threw up among others the major inventions of Savery, Newcomen, and Derby.[3] Thirdly, England was also leading in the commercial field, with a higher volume of trade, both in relation to the population and in absolute terms,[4] with a much larger merchant navy, and with a faster accumulation of merchant capital. Lastly, England's superiority was also very evident in the financial field, where the establishment of the National Debt and the Bank of England were signs of a political and economic structure well in advance of France: attempts by Louis XIV to set up a National Bank foundered on the objections of the bankers who thought it incompatible with a 'pure monarchy', and John Law's attempt a few years later to transplant English financial institutions to France ended in disaster.[5]

In 1688 Gregory King asserted that England had reached a

[1] R. Davis, 'English foreign trade, 1660–1700', *The Economic History Review*, 2nd series, VII (1954), pp. 150–4, 159–63, and 'English foreign trade 1700–1774', ibid., XV (1962), p. 285; D. A. Farnie, 'The commercial empire of the Atlantic, 1607–1783', ibid., XV (1962), p. 206.

[2] F. J. Fisher, in *Economica*, pp. 17–18.

[3] W. H. Chaloner and A. E. Musson, op. cit., p. 33. According to D. C. Coleman in *Past and Present*, XVII, pp. 71–2, it might be possible to speak of an industrial revolution at the end of the seventeenth century.

[4] E. Levasseur, *Histoire du commerce de la France. Première partie: avant 1789* (Paris, 1911), p. 405.

[5] H. Lüthy, *La banque protestante en France, de la révocation de l'édit de Nantes à la Révolution* (Paris, 1959 and 1961, 2 Vols), Vol. I, pp. 94–7, 290–1, 414; R. Mousnier, *Les XVIe et XVIIe siècles* (Paris, 1954), p. 299.

higher level of wealth than any other country, Holland alone excepted, and estimated the French average income per head at 20 per cent lower than the English; a generation later, just after the Treaty of Utrecht, Daniel Defoe was writing of England as 'the most flourishing and opulent country in the world'.[1] These opinions were certainly not unjustified, in view of England's modest but growing prosperity in the seventeenth century, when France was stagnant and even declining. Whatever the causes of this disparity – different socio-economic structures, political circumstances – once the unfavourable economic climate of the seventeenth and early eighteenth centuries had lifted and the French economy started to grow, it was already behind the English and began with a serious handicap. If it is accepted that the Industrial Revolution was merely the crown stage of a long process of growth and change, it is important to our understanding of the British 'take-off' in the last third of the eighteenth century that it came after about two centuries of growth – admittedly broken at times, but never for very long – whereas the growth of the French economy at the same period dated back less than half a century and followed a century of stagnation. It was in fact during this 'tragic' post-1630 seventeenth century that France was clearly outdistanced by England, and despite her relatively fast growth during the eighteenth century she was never able to catch up.

We have seen that the economic developments of France and England during the seventeenth century are in clear contrast; but for the three-quarters of a century between the end of the War of the Spanish Succession and the French Revolution the picture is quite different. In both countries this was a period of growth, and the available statistical data points to the somewhat surprising conclusion that the rates of growth were not at all dissimilar.[2]

Let us start with what is best known, foreign trade, which is

---

[1] Quoted by P. Deane and W. A. Cole, *British Economic Growth, 1688–1959. Trends and Structure* (Cambridge, 1962), p. 38, and M. Ashley, *England in the seventeenth century (1603–1714)* (London, 1952), p. 230.

[2] Naturally, statistics from the eighteenth century can give only rough orders of magnitude or very approximate indexes of development, and they should be used with caution.

also the sector where French growth was fastest – faster in fact than the British. The total foreign trade of England and Wales (imports + exports + re-exports) had an average yearly official value of £13 million for the five years 1716–20 and £31 million for the five years 1784–88, which means it multiplied by 2·4.[1] On the other hand, the average yearly value of France's foreign trade was 215 million livres tournois for 1716–20 and 1 billion 62 millions for 1784–88, which means a fivefold increase.[2] However, the English official values were calculated at more or less constant prices, so that in fact they give a rough index of the volume of trade, while the French figures are at current prices. Since prices rose about 60 per cent between the 1730s and the 1780s, the comparison is only valid if we deflate the figures for 1784–88 to constant prices. But this would still leave an increase in the *volume* of French trade which at lowest is of the order of 1 to 3, and even so is higher than the English. In any case, the value of French foreign trade, which in 1716–20 was barely more than half that of the English, by the eve of the Revolution had reached about the same level (though the value per head of the population was naturally still much lower).[3]

We must, of course, take into account the very low level to which French trade had fallen at the end of the War of the Spanish Succession, but it nevertheless grew faster than the English up to the time of the French Revolution. Moreover, there were several branches of international trade in which the French secured or maintained a dominant position; they continued to be the main suppliers of manufactured goods to Spain, and through Cadiz to Spain's American Empire, while the British had the monopoly of the smaller Portuguese and

---

[1] E. B. Schumpeter, *English Overseas Trade Statistics, 1697–1808* (Oxford, 1960), pp. 15–16, Tables I–IV. Inclusion of Scotland and use of the net imports would not alter this proportion.

[2] A. M. Arnould, *De la balance du commerce et des relations commerciales extérieures de la France dans toutes les parties du globe particulièrement à la fin du règne de Louis XIV et au moment de la Révolution* (Paris, 2nd edn, Year III, 3 vols), Vol. III, Table 10; E. Levasseur, op. cit., p. 512, n. 2.

[3] Moreover, the trade of the great ports such as Bordeaux, Marseilles, and Rouen, grew faster than that of the country as a whole; cf. E. Levasseur, op. cit., pp. 457, 459; P. Dardel, *Navires et marchandises dans les ports du Rouen et du Havre au XVIIIᵉ siècle* (Paris, 1963), pp. 548–51.

Brazilian markets; they dominated the markets of Italy and the Levant. Thanks to spectacular progress in sugar and coffee cultivation in San Domingo and to the low prices of these products, which competed successfully with those of the British West Indies where soils were becoming exhausted and production costs were higher, the French snatched most of the entrepôt trade in colonial produce from the English merchants and developed a large and fast-growing re-export trade to Northern Europe.[1] The British on the whole did not do well in the European markets, where they came up against protective tariffs and French competition. In absolute terms, the increase in English exports to Europe was slow; they did not double between the beginning of the century and the 1780s, and it was only after about 1785 that the products of 'modernized' British industries started to invade the Continent; Europe's share in English total exports also diminished, falling from about four-fifths to under a half. English commercial expansion was due almost entirely to the fast growth of her colonial trade and especially of trade with the American possessions, which up to the revolt of the Thirteen colonies provided English industry with an almost fully protected market.[2] This 'Americanization' of foreign trade is also noticeable, though less marked, in France; French colonial trade, despite losses of territory due to the Seven Years War, grew tenfold between 1716–20 and 1784–88, when trade with countries outside Europe made 38 per cent of total trade. French trade, then, was still more orientated on Europe than the English, and this European trade was growing almost as fast as total trade, certainly faster than that of England with the Continent.[3]

[1] R. Davis, 'English foreign trade, 1700–1774', *The Economic History Review*, 2nd series, xv (1962), p. 294.

[2] Ibid., p. 298; D. A. Farnie, op. cit., p. 214; Deane and Cole, op. cit., pp. 34, 86, 88; E. B. Schumpeter, op. cit., pp. 10–11. Exports to British possessions (including Ireland and the Thirteen colonies) increased sixfold between 1716–20 and 1786–90.

[3] It is true that the main growth in French trade with Europe was made by re-exports (of colonial products) which increased eightfold, while exports of French products barely trebled. Cf. E. Levasseur, op. cit., pp. 487, 512, n. 2; A. M. Arnould, op. cit., Vol. I, pp. 326–7; II, Table 2; III, Table 12; R. Romano, op. cit., pp. 1277, 1291.

This optimistic picture of French foreign trade needs, however, to be qualified on several points. In particular, its relative position seems to have been more favourable during the first half of the period under review, that is before the Seven Years War. Up to the end of the forties, in fact, the development of English trade was 'painfully slow', because of the stagnation in the export of woollen goods and in the re-export; fast growth came only after 1748, with an annual rate of growth of 3·9 per cent between 1745 and 1760. At first, French trade, despite the whiplash of the '*Système*', grew at a rate similar to the English, but after about 1735 it accelerated sooner and faster, doubling in value in under twenty years (between 1736–39 and 1749–55). But this spurt was cut short by the Seven Years War, during which French trade was driven off the seas by the Royal Navy and fell 50 per cent, while English trade continued to grow. Between 1763 and 1771 there was a sharp recovery, whose chief effect, however, was to recover lost ground, and this was followed by distinct stagnation in the 1770s and then an outright recession during the American war. It was only on the very eve of the Revolution that French trade again became buoyant and reached a record level, before collapsing in 1793. English trade on the other hand, despite some slowing down during the 1770s and despite the American crisis, seems to have increased at a slightly faster rate than the French from the time of the Seven Years War and after the peace of 1783 to have picked up very sharply, to make a rapid and sustained growth until the end of the century. There are also signs that the competitive position of French products deteriorated after 1770 and that they were losing ground in the Levant, in Spain (where the protectionist policy of Charles III was a further obstacle) and in Spanish America.[1] In addition, the course of British trade was much less irregular, because it did not suffer as much from the wars.[2]

[1] R. Davis, 'English foreign trade, 1700–1774', op. cit., pp. 285–8, 294–5; E. B. Schumpeter, op. cit., pp. 13–14; Deane and Cole, op. cit., pp. 29–30, 42–9, 310–11; E. Levasseur, op. cit., pp. 511, 521, 523; P. Dardel, op. cit., pp. 49, 51–2, 101–2, 105, 247; E. Labrousse, *La crise de l'économie française à la fin de l'Ancien Régime et au début de la Révolution* (Paris, 1943), pp. xxxvi–xxxix.

[2] But there are also some striking parallels in its development, with alternating

Another weakness of French trade was its great dependence on San Domingo, which in the 1780s was responsible for three-quarters of the trade with the French colonies and also supplied most of the re-exports, which themselves made about one-third of total exports.[1] The proportion of re-exports was almost as great in English trade, but the British colonial empire was larger and more various than the French so that British colonial trade was more diversified; moreover, until 1776 it included as one of its chief markets the Thirteen colonies, with their fast-rising European populations, their relatively high standard of living and expanding demand for manufactured goods of all sorts. Further, the percentage of manufactured goods to total exports was higher in British than in French trade – about two-thirds as against two-fifths in the 1780s; the leading French exports were coffee, sugar, and wines, linen and silk goods taking second place.[2]

However, in France, as in England, commercial expansion was a strategic factor in the growth of industry. This is a more difficult question to discuss, because of the shortage of really satisfactory quantitative materials and the highly conjectural character of the structures which have recently been erected on the shaky foundations of those we possess. For England, W. Hoffmann's index shows that industrial production just trebled between 1700 and 1799; the more recent index of real output in commerce and industry established by Phyllis Deane and W. A. Cole goes up from 100 in 1700 to 285 in 1790, which means an average rate of growth of 1·17 per cent per year; an index of the same type, but for export industries only, rises more sharply during this period, from 100 to 383.[3] For French industry, Jean Marczewski has so far published only some provisional results; according to these, the gross physical product

---

phases of fast growth (between the War of the Austrian Succession and the Seven Years War) and of slow growth or stagnation (after 1713, during the 1770s).

[1] E. Levasseur, *Histoire des classes ouvrières et de l'industrie en France avant 1789* (Paris, 2nd edn 1900, 2 Vols.), Vol. II, pp. 556–7.

[2] E. Levasseur, *Histoire du commerce . . .*, op. cit., pp. 515, 518 n., 521, n. 2.

[3] W. G. Hoffmann, *British Industry, 1700–1950* (Oxford, 1955), Table 54, Part A; Deane and Cole, op. cit., p. 78, Table 19. The index given by these authors refers to the ten-year averages centred on the year quoted.

of French industry and handicraft at current prices rose from a yearly average of 385 million livres for the decade 1701–10 to 1,573 million for 1781–90, which means its volume increased fourfold, in fact at a mean average rate of growth of 1·91 per cent per year.[1] But it seems that fuller and more precise calculations are likely to modify these conclusions, reducing the rate of growth to little more than 1 per cent per year, which would be very close to the figure Deane and Cole obtained for English production. The idea that English and French industrial production increased at much the same pace between the early eighteenth century and the French Revolution may appear surprising, but comparison of the evolution of the main industries in each country appears to bear it out.

As regards the woollen industry, Deane considers that in England its output rose about 150 per cent in the eighteenth century taken as a whole. For France, Pierre Léon puts the increase between the early eighteenth century and 1789 at a mere 60 per cent. But 1789 was a very bad year, and moreover there was a distinct rise in English production during the last decade of the century, so that the disparity in growth between the two industries cannot be as large as the figures might at first suggest. In France the linen industry was very important, in terms of labour force and value of output perhaps bigger than the woollen industry; according to Pierre Léon, its evolution during the eighteenth century went parallel to that of wool. In Britain, linen manufacture was of little importance at the beginning of the eighteenth century and though it later grew fast in Scotland, particularly at mid-century, by national standards it remained a relatively minor activity, and its growth, though sharp, can have had little consequence for industrial output as a whole. As for the silk industry, imports of raw silk into England slightly more than doubled between the beginning of the century and the 1780s, but the English silk industry remained small in comparison with the French, which was growing altogether faster: according to Léon, the number of

---

[1] J. Marczewski, 'Some aspects of the economic growth of France, 1660–1958', *Economic Development and Social Change*, IX, (1961), Tables 1 and 3.

looms at work in Lyons increased 185 per cent between 1720 and 1788.[1]

For cotton, the picture is of course different – but not as different as one would think. There is no need to dwell on its phenomenal growth in Britain. Net imports of raw cotton rose from just over 1 million pounds weight in the early eighteenth century to a yearly figure of over 15 million in 1780–89 (and in this last year to 30 million). However, in France the cotton industry was also growing very fast. J. Marczewski has calculated that its rate of growth between the first and the ninth decades averaged 3·8 per cent per annum; this was similar to the English growth rate but starting initially at a lower level. Thus in 1786 English net imports of cotton were 18 million pounds weight, French only 11 million. This shows the English cotton industry with a definite superiority, but the margin is not so great as it became later. And it must be remembered that until the very last years of the century cotton's contribution to the British national income remained relatively small.[2]

For the mining and metal industries the quantitative data are very unsatisfactory. French coal production was of course much lower than British, but in the eighteenth century it started to grow very fast and by the time of the Revolution had some national importance. As for the iron industry, although there is still much that is obscure and controversial about its evolution in England during the first part of the century, its growth up to about 1760, in fact up to the time of Henry Cort's inventions, was certainly slow; it was only as a result of Cort's

[1] Deane and Cole, op. cit., pp. 52–3, 61, 203, 207; P. Léon, 'L'industrialisation en France en tant que facteur de croissance économique du début du XVIIIe siècle à nos jours', *Première conférence internationale d'histoire économique, Stockholm, 1960* (Paris and The Hague, 1960), pp. 175–6, 178–9. Professor Léon has very kindly supplied additional information, showing in particular that there was a fast growth in the linen industry at St Quentin and in Mayenne (at a time when in Normandy the industry was stagnant).

[2] Deane and Cole, op. cit., pp. 50–2, 163; P. Léon, 'L'industrialisation . . .', op. cit., p. 178; E. Levasseur, *Histoire des classes ouvrières*, op. cit., pp. 524–6, 545, 690; J. Marczewski, op. cit., Table 7; P. Bairoch, *Révolution industrielle et sous-développement* (Paris, 1963), pp. 235–6, 305–7; C. Ballot, *L'introduction du machinisme dans l'industrie française* (Paris, 1923), p. 120; H. Lüthy, op. cit., Vol. II, pp. 663–5; P. Dardel, op. cit., pp. 203, 214, 561.

inventions that iron production showed dramatic increase, doubling in ten years Some figures suggest that until the 1780s output in France grew faster. At all events, on the eve of the Revolution, France probably had an output of from 130,000 to 140,000 tons of pig-iron, as against only 60,000 in England.[1]

This brief survey thus does not contradict the impression left by estimates of global industrial output, and as regards *volume of output*, French industrial performance up to the Revolution compares not unfavourably with the English. France was producing less coal, non-ferrous metals, ships and cotton goods than Britain, but more woollens, linens, and silks, as well as more iron. French total industrial production was appreciably higher than the English, but production per head remained smaller, as it had already been in the seventeenth century.

It is true that in industry, as in foreign trade, French performance seems to have been relatively better in the first half of the period under review than the second. Recovery in output after the depression of the later years of Louis XIV occurred before 1720 in some sectors (Dauphiné, Amiens), after this date in others (Beauvais for example). The recovery was sharp: output of woollens seems to have doubled at Amiens between 1715 and 1750 and trebled at Beauvais between 1724 and 1755. In any case, after 1730 growth was general and quite fast.[2]

---

[1] P. Léon, 'L'industrialisation . . .', op. cit., pp. 177, 179; P. Léon, 'Techniques et civilisations du fer dans l'Europe du XVIIIᵉ siècle', *Le Fer à travers les âges. Hommes et Techniques* (Nancy, 1956) p. 233; B. Gille, 'La metallurgie française d'Ancien Régime', *Revue d'histoire de la sidérurgie*, v (1964), p. 156; H. d'Herouville, 'Réflexions sur la croissance', *Études et conjoncture*, XIII (1958), p. 997; E. F. Heckscher, 'Un grand chapitre de l'histoire du fer: le monopole suédois', *Annales d'Histoire économique et sociale*, IV (1932), p. 132; E. Levasseur, *Histoire des classes ouvrières . . .*, op. cit., Vol. II, p. 675; J. Marczewski, op. cit., Table 8; P. Bairoch, op. cit., pp. 238, 247–8, 313–14; Deane and Cole, op. cit., pp. 55, 221; T. S. Ashton, *An economic history of England. The 18th century* (London, 1955), p. 124; B. R. Mitchell, with the collaboration of P. Deane, *Abstract of British Historical Statistics* (Cambridge, 1962), p. 221; M. W. Flinn, 'The growth of the English iron industry, 1660–1760', *The Economic History Review*, 2nd series, XI (1958), pp. 151–2.

[2] P. Goubert, op. cit., pp. 586, 589; P. Deyon, 'Le mouvement de la production textile à Amiens au XVIIIᵉ siècle', *Revue du Nord*, XLIV (1962), pp. 204, 207; P. Léon, *La naissance de la grande industrie en Dauphiné (fin du XVIIᵉ siècle – 1860)* (Paris, 1954, 2 Vols), Vol. I, pp. 118 ff.

English industrial growth at this period was somewhat sluggish: Deane and Cole observed a faster pace only in the 1740s and 1750s, and even this movement slackened after 1760. Not everyone will agree with this interpretation, but there is no doubt whatever about the violent acceleration during the 1780s in all manufacturing output, which signifies that England had entered on the decisive phase of the Industrial Revolution.[1] Ernest Labrousse has shown that in France there was a slackening in industrial growth from mid-century and after 1770 prolonged stagnation. The old textile industries stopped growing and in some districts – for example Amiens, Normandy, Brittany, and Languedoc – even declined. The agricultural depression around 1780, the worsening lot of the poorer classes, made the difficulties of industry more acute and were a preface to its collapse in 1788–89. These difficulties should not, however, be overestimated, since the stagnation of the old industries (also noticeable in England, where competition from cotton damaged wool and linen) was in part compensated by the fast rise of new industries – cotton in particular, but also coal, iron, glass, and chemical products.[2] However this may be, during the eighteenth century, French industry certainly displayed considerable vitality and buoyancy.[3]

There remains agriculture, a thorny question which cannot be gone into here except to refer to the recent study by J. Toutain which shows for France a 60 per cent increase of the deflated agricultural product between 1701–10 and 1781–90; this growth, somewhat higher than the rise in population, fits in with the disappearance during the eighteenth century of the famines and mass mortalities which had been so frequent in the seventeenth. On the other hand, Deane and Cole have estimated the growth in real output of British agriculture

---

[1] Deane and Cole, op. cit., p. 78, Table 19; T. S. Ashton, *The 18th century*, op. cit., p. 125; A. H. John, 'Aspects of English economic growth in the first half of the eighteenth century', *Economica*, n.s., XXVIII (1961), pp. 176–90.

[2] C. E. Labrousse, *Esquisse du mouvement des prix et des revenus en France au XVIIIe siècle* (Paris, 1933, 2 Vols), pp. 506–8, 548, 555, 557; idem, 'La crise . . .', op. cit., pp. viii, x, xxii–xxiii, xxxii–xxxvii, 177; P. Deyon, 'Le mouvement de la production . . .', op. cit., pp. 207–8; E. Levasseur, *Histoire des classes ouvrières . . .*, op. cit., pp. 527, 682, notes 6 and 7; H. Lüthy, op. cit., Vol. II, p. 594.

[3] P. Léon, 'L'industrialisation . . .', op. cit., p. 179.

between 1700 and 1790 at 35 per cent. These figures are not exactly comparable, but they point, as in the preceding cases, to a roughly parallel growth. Admittedly, English agricultural techniques underwent great improvements during the eighteenth century, for which there is no equivalent in France, but French agriculture was not so conservative as is often thought.[1]

As regards the global growth of the two economies, for Britain the Deane and Cole index of total output rises from 100 in 1700 to 190 in 1790, for France an index of the gross physical product at constant prices, as computed by Marczewski, rises from 100 to 260 between the first and ninth decades of the century, though the last figure may be thought too high.[2] And between 1700 and 1781 the population of France apparently increased 35 per cent (from 19·5 or 20 millions to 26 millions), that of England and Wales only 29 per cent (from 5·8 to 7·5 millions). The growth in average real output and income per head might therefore have been roughly of the same order of magnitude in both countries.[3]

As we have seen, however, at the beginning of the eighteenth century France was behind England, especially as regards the level of average industrial output, foreign trade, and incomes; as both economies grew at about the same rate in the next three-quarters of a century, France could not overtake her rival (although some ground was no doubt made up during the second third of the century), and the close similarity in the rates of growth, which in this paper is deliberately stressed because it has often not been recognized, ought not to disguise the

---

[1] J. C. Toutain, *Le produit de l'agriculture française de 1700 à 1958* (Paris, 1961, 2 Vols, *Histoire quantitative de l'économie française*, Vols I and II), Vol. I, pp. 213, 215; Vol. II, pp. 128 (diagram 110), 133, 136, 139, 204, 276; Deane and Cole, op. cit., p. 78, Table 19; E. Labrousse, *Le paysan* . . ., op. cit., pp. 47–50, 94.

[2] Deane and Cole, op. cit., pp. 78–9; J. Marczewski, 'Some aspects . . .', op. cit., Table 4. In establishing this index, use has been made of some figures of Marczewski which take into account the prevailing relationship between food and manufacturing prices – figures which he considers preferable. On the other hand, P. Bairoch (op. cit., p. 346, diagram 63) has adopted other figures of Marczewski which give only a 69 per cent increase in the total physical output.

[3] J. Toutain, *La population de la France de 1700 à 1959* (Paris, 1963, *Histoire quantitative de l'économie française*, Vol. III), pp. 9, 16; Deane and Cole, op. cit., p. 6, Table 2.

differences between them. In the 1770s England was still the more 'developed', the richer country, with certainly a higher average income per head. England was more urbanized, more industrialized, more involved in international trade; industry employed a higher percentage of the active population and contributed more to national income, roughly over one-quarter, as against one-fifth in France. Moreover, the subsistence sector had virtually disappeared from England as early as the seventeenth century,[1] ousted everywhere by the mercantile and monetary economy; in France the quasi-autarchic subsistence sector was still important and prevailed in extensive areas, acting as a brake on the growth of the economy as a whole.

The fundamental difference between the two economies, however, is in the technological field. The relatively fast expansion of French industry during the eighteenth century took place within a framework which was still, as regards organization and methods, largely the traditional one. Some changes can be observed, for example the tendency towards concentration and growth of commercial capitalism, the migration of industry from the towns to the countryside, the appearance of new products or even of new industries such as cotton, but in general the traditional structures held. On the eve of the Revolution, the French economy was not basically different from what it had been under Louis XIV: it was merely producing much more. In England, on the other hand, where growth during the first half of the century was of the 'French' type, that is, within the traditional framework, after 1760 some revolutionary changes appeared and economic structures were modified in depth by a series of technical inventions which heralded a general revolution.

This is the heart of the matter: Britain was the place where all the basic inventions which created modern industry – the spinning machine, the flying shuttle, the mechanical loom, the printing drum, the coke furnace, puddling, and most revolutionary of all, the steam engine – were made, perfected and introduced into industry. In France inventions were far fewer

---

[1] Deane and Cole, op. cit., pp. 3, 256.

and restricted to improvements for the silk industry (Vaucanson and later Jacquard) and the chemical industry (Berthollet and Leblanc). Eighteenth-century France had some excellent technicians in fields like shipbuilding, ordnance (Gribeauval), and public works, not to mention many marvellous craftsmen, but their talent was not applied to the improvement of industrial techniques. French industry only developed on the technical side through taking up foreign machines and techniques, and to assimilate them usually required the help of foreign technicians, most of them British, though some were Swiss or German.[1]

England experienced a real outburst of inventiveness, which in France was almost completely lacking, and this decisive British superiority in ingenuity and willingness to innovate is the basic fact which has accentuated the structural discrepancy between the two economies during the second part of the eighteenth century, and which we must now try to explain.

This is a difficult task, all the more so because the foregoing analysis has removed one convenient explanation: if, as is sometimes believed, British output had increased much faster than the French, British inventiveness could then very easily be explained as a function, a by-product, of growth. But as things are, the parallel growth in output in the two countries makes the British superiority harder to understand, since there seems nothing specific or unique about the development of the English economy, or at least of a large part of it. And in so far as individual genius remains something of a mystery, it will never be fully explained why England had so many great inventors in the eighteenth century. All the historian can hope for is to understand the environment which favoured the making of inventions and which made manufacturers eager to take them up.

The earliest economic historians, when they considered this question, attached great importance to the English institutional framework. Efforts by the State to control and regulate indus-

---

[1] See particularly P. Léon, 'Tradition et machinisme dans la France du XVIIIe siècle', *Information Historique*, XVII (1955), pp. 5–14.

try had been abandoned as early as the seventeenth century, and though the relevant laws were still theoretically in force, they were never applied; at the same time, the guild system had fallen into decay.[1] Eighteenth-century England was thus a country of *laissez-faire*, in which the field was left free for individual initiative. In France, on the other hand, the guilds survived and their members resisted the development of large-scale enterprises and the introduction of new techniques. Moreover, Colbertist regulations, by prescribing detailed standards of workmanship, discouraged innovations. And in England, such vestiges of corporate regulation and public control as did survive, as for example in the woollen industry, had precisely the effect of encouraging routinism.

Historians like Levasseur, however, went too far in envisaging eighteenth-century French industry as imprisoned in the double straight-jacket of guilds and regulations, which they saw as an insuperable barrier to progress and the reason why French inventions were so few.[2] Nowadays, it is accepted that the guild system was never general in France and in fact did not apply to the greater part of industry; it was unknown in the economic life of many towns, for example Lyons, in royal manufactures, in rural domestic industries, and in new industries such as cotton.[3] Moreover, the system went into rapid decline in the second half of the century, as did Colbertist regulations, which had always been evaded and which from mid-century were less and less strictly enforced, as governmental circles were converted to *laissez-faire* policies. The contrast between French 'dirigism' and English liberalism should thus not be overestimated and it seems that the influence of the institutional framework, though real, was limited.

Some recent historians have stressed the importance of socio-psychological factors, involving a distinct contrast between the English and French social structures and 'scales of

[1] T. S. Ashton, *The Industrial Revolution*, op. cit., pp. 11–12.
[2] E. Levasseur, *Histoire des classes ouvrières . . .*, op. cit., Vol. II, p. 305. And A. Toynbee and W. Cunningham also overestimated the influence of *laissez-faire* on the English side.
[3] But the rise of this industry was certainly delayed by the prohibitions against printed cottons which remained in force until 1759.

value' to explain the British superiority in inventiveness and the entrepreneurial spirit.[1] These writers have shown, with justice, that there was greater vertical social mobility in eighteenth-century England than in France, but it is odd that they should emphasize an aspect of the problem which seems both disputable and of secondary importance. They maintain that in England the social barrier separating the great landed classes from industry and commerce, the barrier, that is, between the aristocracy and the business world, was relatively low. But this can have very little bearing on the problem, since the Industrial Revolution was certainly not the work of the British aristocracy nor even of the gentry. As we know, England had the Duke of Bridgewater and his canal and some great landowners who took an interest in business, but on the whole active participation and investment in industry by the nobility and gentry seems to have actually declined during the eighteenth century, notably in metallurgy. Moreover, despite the contrary assertions of some English-speaking sociologists, the French nobility was not a close caste, nor was it totally uninterested in business. It controlled a good part of the metallurgical and glass industries and the coal-mines; it invested in foreign trading ventures and West Indian plantations, and on the eve of the Revolution a number of *grands seigneurs* like the Duke of Orleans and the Count of Artois were active in enterprises concerned to introduce English technology into France.

No one, however, will deny that the social prestige of business was lower in France than in England, that the ideal of *vivre noblement* (that is of doing nothing) was stronger there, contempt for work more widespread. But here, too, caution is necessary. For example, writers have often stressed that the French bourgeois who got rich in business retired from it as soon as possible to buy land or public office. And the sale of offices has been rightly criticized as an important factor in diverting capital and talents away from productive activities (tax-farming and financial deals with a government perpetually

---

[1] T. S. Ashton, *The 18th Century*, op. cit., pp. 20–1; D. S. Landes, 'Encore le problème de la Révolution industrielle en Angleterre', *Bulletin de la société d'histoire moderne*, 12th series, *18*, p. 7.

hard up played the same role). But this factor was much less important in the eighteenth than in the seventeenth century, as the State was no longer resorting to mass creations and sales of offices. As for the diversion of capital to land, this was also a marked feature in England, where it was the dream of every merchant who got rich to become a country gentleman: and though he himself often retained an interest in the business which had made his fortune, it very rarely survived into the next generation.

As regards our present problem, vertical mobility and scales of values may well be less important than differences between the two countries in the mentality of the men actually engaged in business. In English society there was a more 'capitalist', a more commercial, a more acquisitive spirit; and according to contemporary accounts there was in England a harshness, a ruthlessness, a concentration on the pursuit of gain, which was absent in the more easy-going France of the Ancien Régime. Yet the French social and psychological environment was not basically hostile to innovation, and many manufacturers were quite ready to take up foreign inventions (although they often had difficulty in making them work). French merchants too, displayed plenty of initiative and daring in overseas ventures. In any case, such observations are primarily descriptive and quite superficial, leaving the differences in the two mentalities unaccounted for.

Basically, the problem is still obscure and new research is needed into the relationship between the English and French social structures on the one hand and the entrepreneurial mentalities and attitudes on the other. What is most needed is a close analysis at the local or regional level, since to speak of English society and French society as a whole only leaves one with dubious generalities. After all, the Industrial Revolution was not made in England but in a few small districts of England – south Lancashire, some sectors of the East Midlands and Yorkshire, Birmingham, and the Black Country. The inventors and innovators were recruited from the middle class of these industrial districts, from the merchant-manufacturers and the skilled, well-to-do artisans, and England's wealth in qualified cadres of this type was certainly an important factor.[1] A detailed comparison between these English nurseries of the Industrial Revolution and some French industrial centres would be very instructive. Another pointer is the fact that most of the English discoveries were the product of joint effort, as for example with the notable collaboration of Black, Watt, Boulton and Wilkinson over the steam engine;[2] in France, a larger and more rural country, an element of isolation may have hampered this type of co-operation and cross-stimulus.

Another difficult question is the influence of the Enlightenment. The relationship between the Industrial Revolution and the English philosophical and scientific movement of the late seventeenth century and the eighteenth century is well known. Recent research has stressed the importance of the belief, which goes back to Newton, that industrial progress was possible through observation and experiment; it has shown that most of the inventions (although largely the work of practical men with little education) were backed by systematic thinking, that British scientists and manufacturers were often in close contact, for example in bodies such as the Birmingham Lunar Society, and that scientific knowledge had penetrated industrial society down to a very modest level.[3] But the philosophical and scientific movement was at least as powerful in France, which had plenty of scientists, some of whom, like Buffon and Réaumur, tried their hand at industrial research; scientific societies and academies existed there in profusion and numbered business men among their members; belief in progress and the wish to improve man's material condition were at least as widespread as in England, and Diderot's *Encylopédie* is striking proof of the interest cultivated people took in technology. But unlike what happened in England, all this intellectual

---

[1] See the excellent comments of A. H. John (op. cit., pp. 188–9) on the increase to their numbers because of the prosperity prevailing in the first half of the century.

[2] T. S. Ashton, *The Industrial Revolution*, op. cit., pp. 14, 69; *The 18th Century*, op. cit., p. 105.

[3] T. S. Ashton, *The Industrial Revolution*, op. cit., pp. 14, 16; A. E. Musson and E. Robinson, 'Science and industry in the late eighteenth century', *The Economic History Review*, 2nd series, XIII (1960), pp. 222–44.

activity had very little practical result; discussions in learned societies remained theoretical in character and those who took part lacked a sense of the concrete.[1] A study of this question which also took education into account would again be very useful. In Britain, dissenters and Scotsmen played a major role in the Industrial Revolution because, thanks to the dissenting academies and the much more advanced Scottish educational system,[2] they were the best-educated section of the middle class. French businessmen had either a very elementary or a purely classical education. This difference may have had important consequences.

To sum up, although neither the differences in social structure and mentality between the two countries in the eighteenth century nor the features of the English social environment which favoured the entrepreneurial spirit should be minimized, the contrast does not appear to be as sharp as is often said. Moreover, the real influence of such concrete differences as did exist is still obscure, and though they may in some respects account for British technical superiority, they can only be a secondary factor in comparison with strictly economic forces. After all, technical progress is closely bound up with economic phenomena, and the explanation we are looking for must be first and foremost an economic one.[3] The contention is that the French did not innovate because, unlike the British, they were not made to do so by the strong pressure of economic forces.

Did this pressure arise from demand? Several writers have maintained that a fast growth in the demand for manufactured goods from both the home and the export markets presented British industry with a challenge it could meet only by a technical revolution. This is an attractive hypothesis, but its major premise, that there was an abnormally fast growth in demand in eighteenth-century England is still unproved, and in any

[1] I am grateful to my friend and colleague Louis Trénard for useful suggestions on this point.

[2] T. S. Ashton, *The Industrial Revolution*, op. cit., pp. 17, 19, 20.

[3] J. Schmookler, 'Economic sources of inventive activity', XXII (1962), pp. 1–2.

case there seems no reason why effective global demand should have grown much faster in England than in France.

Population growth in the two countries was of the same order, and anyway there was a comparable upsurge in population throughout Western Europe around mid-century. Recently there has been much debate about the relationship between the industrial and demographic revolutions, but some of the contributors are surely right in stressing that while population growth was doubtless a necessary condition for the Industrial Revolution, it was by no means a sufficient or decisive one, since it was general throughout Western Europe.

Turning to average real incomes per head, they certainly rose in England during the first half of the eighteenth century, when the population was almost stationary, food prices falling, and money wages rising; the internal market therefore expanded, consumption of many articles increased, there was a broadening in range and improvement in quality; A. H. John has pointed out that this permanently affected the level of consumption in most classes and even aroused an appetite for mass consumption. This progress, however, did not last, for from mid-century the expansion of the economy was absorbed by the upsurge in population, and average output per head only started to grow again in the 1780s.[1] But development in France seems to have been roughly parallel, with a rise in average incomes during the first half of the century followed by a degree of stagnation. Labrousse has shown that from the 1760s food prices and rents were certainly rising faster than money wages, which means a fall in real wages, affecting not only the urban wage-earner and the landless rural proletariat but also many poor peasants with some land of their own, who derived part of their income from wages; a large section of the population therefore became poorer, and this must have meant a fall in its average consumption of manufactured goods. However, the rise in rents and agricultural profits was at the same time enriching a not insignificant part of the population, not only the 'feudal' landlords but also the well-to-do peasants. This was a

[1] T. S. Ashton, *The 18th Century*, op. cit., p. 232; A. H. John, op. cit., pp. 180–3, 190; Deane and Cole, op. cit., pp. 18–19, 21, 41, 80–1.

stimulus to trade, and in particular trade in colonial products, and to industry and urban development, and produced a rise in non-agricultural incomes. There is therefore no reason why average effective demand for manufactured goods should have decreased, except possibly during the late 1770s and the 1780s when according to Labrousse the fall in food prices brought about a general stagnation.[1] But, and this is the important point, the slowing down in French demand would have come only after the English had made their great innovations, which were put into effect during a period of prosperity on both sides of the Channel.

There is also the demand from foreign markets to consider. In both countries it was more elastic and increased much faster than internal consumption (although it absorbed a much smaller proportion of output); but as we have already seen, British exports of manufactures increased no faster than French, with the important exception of cotton goods.[2] In addition it must be said, against a currently held opinion, that French losses of colonial territories as a result of the Seven Years War had little effect on exports, since few French goods were taken up by the Canadian and Indian markets, which were only of potential value; nor did England derive much immediate advantage from her conquests.[3]

In fact, the important differences between the English and French markets for manufactured goods are to be observed in their structure rather than their evolution.

In the first place, the British home market – unlike the French – was a truly national market, since the country was an economic unity and there were no internal customs or tolls. This factor should not be overstressed, since the principal French customs unit – the 'Five big Farms' – covered a population about as

[1] E. Labrousse, *Esquisse*, op. cit., Vol. II, pp. 379, 382–3, 444, 497, 598–9, 610–11, 617; *La crise* . . ., op. cit., pp. xxv–xxviii, xxxi; *Le paysan* . . ., op. cit., pp. 4–5, 66, 78 ff., 86, 91, 97.

[2] E. B. Schumpeter, op. cit., p. 12; Deane and Cole, op. cit., p. 59; see also *Past and Present*, XVII, p. 74, and K. Berrill, 'International trade and the rate of economic growth', *The Economic History Review*, 2nd series, XII (1960), p. 358 which stresses the importance of England's capture of the expanding market for this article of mass consumption.

[3] Deane and Cole, op. cit., p. 85, n. 2.

large as Britain. Nevertheless, as K. Berrill has rightly stressed, during the eighteenth century Britain and her colonies formed the largest 'free trade area' in the world. Furthermore, the small size of the country, its configuration, and the early improvement to its transport, contributed to making this national market a reality and internal circulation much more active than in France.[1]

Again, demand within this market was more intense, because as we have already seen, from the beginning of the eighteenth century Britain had a higher average income per head and a higher standard of living. There is no doubt at all that the British masses were better fed, better clothed, better shod than their French counterparts; the percentage of really poor in the total population may have been smaller and that of well-to-do middle-class people greater. In consequence, if average demand for manufactured goods did not grow faster than in France, it still kept to a higher level for the whole of the period under review.[2]

Lastly, the pattern of consumption was also different, though not in the sense often claimed. Some English-speaking writers maintain that France had only luxury industries such as silk, crystals, porcelain, cabinet-making, which were unsuited to machine production, while England specialized early in making cheap goods for a mass market, which could be mass-produced by machinery in factories.[3] France certainly had luxury or semi-luxury industries which catered for the upper classes; their relative importance was greater than in England and they were little suited to mechanization. But in addition France had large industries which catered for popular consumption, turning out coarse woollens and linens for the peasantry, for West Indian slaves and for the Spanish colonies. Now this production for the masses was not large-scale mass production, since the market was fragmented and the places of manufacture dispersed; moreover, it catered for an unfastidious clientèle and

---

[1] K. Berrill, op. cit., p. 358; A. H. John, op. cit., pp. 185–8.
[2] D. S. Landes, op. cit., p. 6. Some absurd objections included in the discussion of Landes' paper may safely be ignored.
[3] *Past and Present*, XVII, pp. 79–80; G. N. Clark, op. cit., pp. 169–70.

used very cheap rural labour, so there was no pressing need to make technical improvements. On the other hand, it appears that British superiority in the eighteenth century was in the manufacture of good quality products suitable for middle-class consumption; and when Frenchmen complained (at any rate before the 1780s) about British competition, they stressed the superior quality, finish and appearance of the goods manufactured in Britain. In part the contrast was a reflection of the differing social structures of the two countries and their colonies: England, relatively speaking, had a larger middle class and the fast-growing population of the Thirteen colonies had a standard of living close to that of the middle classes in Europe. English industry was therefore not catering for a true 'mass market' – this appeared only in the nineteenth century – but only for a mass market in embryo, among above all the middle classes. But in the result output had to be both somewhat standardized and of good quality, which undoubtedly encouraged increased division of labour and technical improvements in order to keep prices low, and also the concentration of work in factories, to maintain quality by better supervision.[1]

We may also wonder whether the growth in demand for manufactured goods was not more regular in England than in France, where recurrent crises and wars were more serious interruptions. T. S. Ashton has pointed out that in England the number of patents rose during periods of expansion and optimism and decreased during depressions or wars. Therefore if economic fluctuations were much more violent in France, this could have had a discouraging effect on innovation. Since it is generally agreed that short-term fluctuations in eighteenth-century industrial output were due mainly to variations in harvest yields, a comparison of fluctuations in grain prices on both sides of the Channel would undoubtedly be of interest. We have nothing for England to set beside the great work of Labrousse, so comparison can only be summary and superficial, based on price series which are not truly comparable. One has

---

[1] The pattern of English consumption was also undoubtedly more 'advanced', textiles having less predominance and metal goods, pottery, etc., greater relative importance.

M

the impression, however, that in the eighteenth century, unlike the seventeenth, the amplitude of such fluctuations was not noticeably more violent in France than in England.[1]

As for fluctuations in output, it is known that in some centres in France production fell about 50 per cent in the course of a cycle, but such cases are exceptional. In England two reasonably well-founded manufacturing series, one for printed goods and the other for West Riding cloth, show that in several cases output fell 20 per cent or even 25 per cent in the course of a given cycle.[2] As a hypothesis, we might conclude that fluctuations were less violent than in France, probably because a larger proportion of output was intended for export, so that in a year of bad harvest the foreign, and especially the non-European, demand was more likely to compensate for the fall on the home market.

The impact of the wars of the eighteenth century has recently stimulated some interesting debates among British historians: for them the problem centres on whether their favourable effects – such as encouraging output and technical innovation in the metal industries – were outweighed by their depressive effects on other branches of the economy.[3] For France the question hardly arises, since there is no doubt that the balance was unfavourable in view of the very serious interruption to seaborne trade during hostilities. Admittedly, out of the three wars the only really disastrous one for France was the Seven Years War. But whatever the outcome of particular battles and the conditions of peace, in time of war the Royal Navy was always in command of the seas, leaving France, despite the use of neutral ships, to a large extent cut off from overseas countries

[1] The divergence between average minimum and maximum yearly prices within one cycle is in the worst cases of the order of 1 to 2 – while in seventeenth-century France it was 1 to 3 or 4. But in most of the cycles the amplitude of the movement was much less.

[2] E. Labrousse, *Esquisse*, op. cit., Vol. II, p. 549; *La crise . . .*, op. cit., p. xl; P. Deyon, 'Le mouvement de la production . . .', op. cit., p. 211; T. S. Ashton, *The 18th Century*, op. cit., pp. 248–9.

[3] A. H. John, 'Wars and the English economy, 1700–1763', *The Economic History Review*, 2nd series, VII (1955), pp. 329–44; T. S. Ashton, *The Industrial Revolution*, op. cit., pp. 90–1; *The 18th Century*, op. cit., pp. 126–7; *Economic Fluctuations in England, 1700–1800* (Oxford, 1959), pp. 69–83.

and particularly her colonies. The British sea lanes, on the other hand, were kept open and British commerce, despite French privateering, had real protection. French trade thus fell sharply during each of the wars, though the worst collapse was naturally during the Seven Years War, when its annual average was barely half that of the preceding years; even so, the situation was little better during the American war; only the War of the Austrian Succession was without really adverse effects. The fall in French exports caused a decline in industrial activity but from Labrousse's figures, the recession was not so great as in foreign trade, which is normal since the greater part of industrial output was distributed on the home market. The adverse influence of the wars should therefore not be overstressed, and indeed H. Lüthy and A. Rémond have maintained that on the whole France was fairly prosperous during the Seven Years War.[1] On the other hand, while English foreign trade rose significantly during the Seven Years War, it fell during the War of the Austrian Succession and fell badly (although less than the French) during the American war. A relationship might be seen between the innovations of the 1760s and the optimism, the confidence in expansion, aroused by England's crushing victories; yet the disaster of American independence was immediately followed by acceleration in the rate of economic growth. On the whole, British maritime and colonial victories do not appear to have been important factors in British technical superiority; it was only during the Revolutionary and Napoleonic wars that complete command of the seas gave Britain the monopoly of overseas markets as a powerful stimulus to growth.[2]

There are, then, a number of interesting divergences to be noted between the character and evolution of demand for

[1] E. Labrousse, *Esquisse*, op. cit., Vol. II, p. 548; E. Levasseur, *Histoire des classes ouvrières* . . ., op. cit., Vol. II, p. 551, n. 2; H. Lüthy, op. cit., Vol. II, pp. 12, 42–4, 357–8; P. Dardel, op. cit., pp. 49–50, 249–51, 257, 516; A. Rémond, 'Trois bilans de l'économie française au temps des théories physiocratiques', *Revue d'histoire économique et sociale*, xxxv (1957), pp. 420–1.

[2] H. J. Habakkuk, *American and British technology in the nineteenth century. The search for labour-saving inventions* (Cambridge, 1962), pp. 185–6. However, there is need for a study in depth of the role of the navy as an outlet for industry and eventually as a stimulus to technical progress.

manufactures in France and England; but these appear less important than those to be observed on the supply side of industry, in the analysis of productive factors.

The Industrial Revolution was not something gratuitous, a triumph of technical progress for its own sake, but a determined effort to solve some concrete problems facing British industry; the character of the most significant inventions reveals what those problems were. The inventions were designed to make possible the replacement of relatively scarce and expensive resources, such as wood, water power, and labour by others which were relatively plentiful and cheap, such as coal, steam power, and capital, the last in the form of labour-saving machines and processes.[1] This underlying character reflects the fact that English industry in the eighteenth century suffered from relative shortages, particularly of fuel in the iron industry and of labour in textile manufactures, and that such bottle-necks were hampering expansion in output. In other words, unless a technical breakthrough was achieved, the available productive factors were inadequate (except through an excessive rise in prices) to meet the relatively fast increase in demand which started in mid-century when the population growth made itself felt. The contention is that these shortages and bottle-necks, which in England exerted strong pressure in favour of innovation, did not exist in France.

In the primary iron industry the contrast is quite evident. Admittedly, we must not overestimate the wood 'famine' which some writers say existed in England as early as the seventeenth century. Michael Flinn has shown recently that between 1550 and 1750 charcoal prices rose little higher than prices in general, and that ironmasters could secure a fuel supply either by systematic copse 'cultivation' or by moving their works to remote and wooded districts. Even so, in any region, every attempt to increase output meant a fast rise in marginal costs, so that prospects for expansion were limited. On the other hand, from the sixteenth century coal had been cheaper than

[1] T. S. Ashton, *The 18th Century*, op. cit., pp. 108–9; *The Industrial Revolution*, op. cit., p. 91.

charcoal in terms of heat output per unit. The ironmasters were aware of the economic advantages of coal, and they also knew that vast reserves of it lay hidden underground. There was therefore a strong incentive to look for methods allowing the substitution of coal for charcoal in blast furnaces, a search which began in the sixteenth century. When it had been successful, by the early eighteenth century, ironmasters who wished to take advantage of the growing demand for iron, were induced increasingly to replace charcoal, which was expensive and limited in supply, by coke, which was a cheaper and much more elastic source; eventually, in the last quarter of the century, ironmasters found they either had to go over to coke smelting or close down. Technical progress therefore resulted from the pressure of growing demand on inadequate wood resources, and this explains why coke smelting was discovered and taken up in England rather than in countries where supplies of wood were cheaper and more elastic.[1] In France, where large forests were still extant, the situation was quite different, and though there was some pressure on wood resources during the eighteenth century and prices rose sharply,[2] such shortages as developed remained purely local and French ironmasters were never faced with the choice between innovation or extinction; and in France coal was scarce and expensive.

Moreover, in England the growing demand for coal for both industrial and domestic purposes during the eighteenth century led to deeper working of the mines, which created the need for more efficient pumping devices; and this of course was a powerful incentive in the development of the steam engines, which was in fact a by-product of the rise of the British coal industry. The same incentive was lacking in France, because of the different balance between wood and coal resources.

---

[1] M. W. Flinn, 'Timber and the advance of technology: a reconsideration', *Annals of Science*, xv (1959), pp. 109–20.

[2] According to E. Labrousse, *Esquisse*, op. cit., Vol. II, pp. 346–7, the price of wood for burning increased 91 per cent between 1726–41 and 1785–9; but the substantial rise occurred after 1770; this had to do with wood intended for domestic use, and in any case the price of wood represented only a small part of the cost price of iron, whose prices certainly did not follow the rise in wood prices.

A contrast between France and England is also evident in the textile industry, but here it is in the supply of labour. The putting out system (domestic labour allied with commercial capitalism) which prevailed in the industry had many advantages, but also the disadvantage that expansion of output was hampered by rising marginal costs. Once the development of an industrial centre had passed a certain limit, to increase production work had to be put out over an ever-widening area, and at a period when communications were slow this meant increased distribution costs, which were soon exceeding profits; the worker spent too much time going to and fro; supervision of the work was becoming impossible and the risks of bad workmanship and of embezzlement of the raw materials were growing. Putting out could, of course, be concentrated on a restricted area where the workers could be made to work longer and faster, but such attempts were thwarted by a regressive labour supply, since the bait of increased earnings was not enough to lure the worker away from his traditional way of life, with its leisure hours and convivial drinking sessions.

There is plentiful evidence of the appearance of this kind of situation during the first half of the eighteenth century in a number of English industrial districts where the putting-out system had developed early and was widespread, with the result that all available labour within reasonable reach of each centre was used up. Nor was there an unlimited supply of mobile labour: the innovations in agriculture, far from creating unemployment were stimulating demand for labour, which contradicts the older view that England was at this period suffering from large-scale rural underemployment and that there was a mass exodus from the countryside to the industrial centres. We must also remember that up to mid-century the population grew only very slowly. Although it then started growing fast, a number of years had to pass before a large supply of hands was available for the labour market, and by this time demand was again increasing. There was therefore a relative shortage of labour in industrial districts, as is proved by the quite sharp rise in money wages there (not found in the south of England) during the first half of the eighteenth century.

Manufacturers were therefore faced with high and rising labour costs, which was particularly embarrassing in a young industry like cotton, which in practice had to build up its labour force at the expense of the older industries. There must therefore have been great difficulty during the 1750s in meeting the fast-growing demand for cottons, particularly for export to the colonies. But in the 1760s and 1770s, when there was some slackening in demand, the rise in manufacturing costs was really dangerous. It was now imperative to reduce labour costs and therefore to invent and take up labour-saving machinery. The relative shortage of labour which affected English industry seems therefore to have been one of the most powerful incentives to innovation, not only in the cotton industry but in several others as well.

In France the situation is again obviously different. The countryside was relatively less industrialized, the relaxation of the regulations against rural manufactures, (especially after the suspension of 1762) freed vast reserves of labour, and this meant it was possible to put work out in a wider area around the industrial centres without unduly increasing labour costs. Moreover, since the rise in the French population was due solely to a fall in deaths (whereas in England there was also an increase in births) in France the number of people of working age may have grown faster. Lastly, and most important, there was in the French countryside a large pool of semi-employed proletarians which putters-out could use without bringing pressure on wages.[1] Labrousse has shown that this proletariat increased fast during the eighteenth century, outpacing the agricultural demand for labour and glutting the labour market.

In sum, during the first half of the eighteenth century, industrial growth in England had reached limits not to be crossed without a technological breakthrough, which the increase in population and in demand from the 1740s made imperative. In France, on the other hand, there was no shortage of labour, output could be increased to meet demand without looking for drastic innovations. This may rank as the most

[1] E. Labrousse, *Esquisse*, op. cit., Vol. II, pp. 491–2, 598–9; *La crise . . .*, op. cit., pp. xxix–xxxi.

important of the differences to be observed between England and France, but it was in part due to England's earlier and more intense industrialization, and hence to the situation in the seventeenth century.

There remains the question of capital resources. In eighteenth-century England capital was relatively abundant, as is shown by the fall in interest rates over a long period; Ashton saw this as the deciding factor in the Industrial Revolution, but most British historians have not followed him.[1] In any case, there was the same fall in interest rates in France. From what little we know about the financing of French industry in the eighteenth century there is nothing to suggest that its development was hampered by a shortage of capital resources[2] – especially at a time when industrial investment had a very low threshold and the earliest spinning jennies, for example, could be got for a few pounds sterling. We know, of course, that the English banking system was much more advanced than the French, but the banks played only a minor and indirect part in financing the Industrial Revolution: industries for the most part financed themselves, through ploughing back profits.[3] However, in England capital accumulation was at a faster rate than the growth of other factors in production, especially labour supplies, and this was a powerful incentive to innovation. Things may have been different in France, but this could only be proved by research into the problem, which has not yet been done.

This analysis, which could be accused of being both too long and too general, may appear inconclusive because in many cases it has tried to play down the 'sharp contrasts' between the French and English economies dear to the textbooks, contrasts which have been given too readily as the explanation for

[1] T. S. Ashton, *The Industrial Revolution*, op. cit., pp. 11, 58, 94.

[2] For a different view see H. Lüthy, op. cit., Vol. II, p. 41, and C. Fohlen in his Introduction to the French edition of T. S. Ashton, *The Industrial Revolution* (Paris, 1955), pp. xvi–xviii.

[3] F. Crouzet, 'La formation du capital en Grande-Bretagne pendant la Révolution industrielle', *Deuxième conférence internationale d'histoire économique. Aix-en-Provence. 1962* (Paris and The Hague, 1965), Vol. II, pp. 598 ff.

Britain's superior inventiveness and economic lead. There is no wish to deny that differences existed between the two countries, though many seem to have been less pronounced than is generally thought, and a matter of degree rather than kind. What is important is that these differences nearly all point in the same direction: in all the various fields investigated, in England the conditions for innovation seem to have been more favourable than in France.[1] The accumulation of these relative differences, many of them small but very important as regards factors such as fuel and labour supplies, seems to have been sufficient to set in motion a cumulative and self-sustaining process of technical advance; in France there was no such movement, because there was no need for it. In a paper read in Paris in 1961, David Landes used an illuminating metaphor borrowed from nuclear physics: he spoke of a 'critical mass', a piling up of various factors favouring England's growth which triggered off a chain reaction – the Industrial Revolution.[2] In France, on the other hand, there was no such critical mass, which is why France did not start spontaneously an Industrial Revolution. The external stimulus of serious competition from cheaper English goods, first in foreign markets and after the treaty of 1786 in France itself, was needed to set in train a number of French efforts, intensified during the 1780s, which aimed at introducing the new English technology into France. At this date English industry had a clear superiority, but was only just entering the stage of fast growth and widespread revolutionary changes; France was not disastrously behind, and the Industrial Revolution might have taken off there with only a few years' delay in relation to England. But the 'national catastrophe' which the French Revolution and the twenty years war meant to the French economy[3] would intensify the discrepancy and make it irremediable. In 1815 it would be more

---

[1] Of course, many of these differences had deep historical roots, and for example, the contrast between the English and French colonial markets has its origin in the settlement of the English in Virginia and Massachusetts and of the French in Canada and San Domingo.

[2] D. S. Landes, op. cit., p. 6.

[3] M. Lévy-Leboyer, *Les banques européennes et l'industrialisation internationale dans la première moitié du XIXe siècle* (Paris, 1964), p. 29.

pronounced than in 1789, because during this quarter of a century, despite a delaying effect due to the wars, the British economy had continued to change and to make rapid growth.[1]

[1] See F. Crouzet, *L'Économie britannique et le Blocus continental (1806–1813)* (Paris, 1958, 2 Vols), Vol. II, pp. 863–72; 'Les conséquences économiques de la Révolution. A propos d'un inédit de Sir Francis d'Ivernois', *Annales historiques de la Révolution française*, 34th year, nos. 168 and 169, 1962, pp. 182–217, 336–62; 'Wars, blockade and economic change in Europe, 1792–1815', *Journal of Economic History*, XXIV (1964), pp. 567–88; 'Bilan de l'économie britannique pendant les guerres de la Révolution et de l'Empire', *Revue Historique*, no. 475, July–September 1965, pp. 71–110.

Select Bibliography

References to many books and articles will be formal in the Editor's introductory chapter, and in all other chapters, especially Chapter 7. The following bibliography mentions only some of the more important sources for studying the causes of the industrial revolution and the process of economic growth in eighteenth-century England. Books and articles of a general character which sum up the research and literature of particular subjects have been especially selected. Most of the books and articles in Section I are also relevant for the subjects of the other sections.

I *General Explanations of Industrialization*

ASHTON, T. S. *The Industrial Revolution* (1948).
   An Economic History of England: The 18th Century (1955).
BEALES, H. L. *The Industrial Revolution, 1752–1850* (rev. edn 1958).
DEANE P. and COLE, W. A. *British Economic Growth, 1688–1959 Trends and Structure* (1962), Ch. 2.
DEANE, P. *The First Industrial Revolution* (1965).
DEANE P. and HABAKKUK, H. J. 'The Take-off in Britain', *The Economics of Take-off into Sustained Growth* (1963).
FLINN, M. W. *Origins of the Industrial Revolution* (1966).
GERSCHENKRON, A. 'Reflections on the Concept of "Prerequisites" of Modern Industrialization', *Economic Backwardness in Historical Perspective* (1962).
HARTWELL, R. M. *The Industrial Revolution* (Historical Association Pamphlet No. 58, 1965).
   'Economic Change in England and Europe, 1780–1830', *The New Cambridge Modern History*, Vol. IX (1965), pp. 31–48.
JOHN, A. H. 'Aspects of English Economic Growth in the First Half of the Eighteenth Century', *Economica* (1961).
LANDES, D. 'Technological Change and Development in

Western Europe, 1750–1914', *The Cambridge Economic History of Europe*, Vol. VI (1965), pp. 274–352.

NEF, J. U. 'The Industrial Revolution Reconsidered', *The Journal of Economic History* (1943).

ROSTOW, W. W. 'The Take-off into self-sustained growth', *Economic Journal* (1956).

WILSON, C. *England's Apprenticeship, 1603–1763* (1966).

II *Population Growth*

CIPOLLA, C. *The Economic History of World Population* (1962).

GLASS, D. V. and EVERSLEY, D. E. C. *Population in History. Essays in Historical Demography* (1965), Part II.

III *Agricultural Change*

CHAMBERS, J. D. and MINGAY, G. E. *The Agricultural Revolution, 1750–1880* (1966).

JONES, E. L. (ed.), *Agriculture and Economic Growth in England, 1650–1815* (1967).

IV *Transport Development*

JACKMAN, W. T. *The Development of Transportation in Modern England* (1916).

SAVAGE, C. F. *An Economic History of Transport* (1959).

V *Trade*

DAVIS, R. 'English Foreign Trade, 1660–1700' and 'English Foreign Trade, 1700–1774', *The Economic History Review* (1954 and 1962).

SCHLOTE, W. *British Overseas Trade from 1700 to the 1930's* (1952).

SCHUMPETER, E. B. *British Overseas Trade Statistics, 1696–1782* (1961).

VI *Management*

POLLARD, S. *The Genesis of Modern Management. A Study of the Industrial Revolution in Great Britain* (1965).

WILSON, C. 'The Entrepreneur in the Industrial Revolution', *History* (1957).

VII *Technology*

MUSSON, A. E. and ROBINSON, E. 'Science and Industry in the Late Eighteenth Century',. *The Economic History Review* (1960).
SINGER, CHARLES and OTHERS *A History of Technology* (5 vols, 1954–58), Vol. V.

VIII *Labour*

CHAMBERS, D. 'Enclosure and Labour Supply during the Industrial Revolution', *The Economic History Review* (1953).
COATS, A. W. 'Changing Attitudes to Labour in the Mid-eighteenth Century', *The Economic History Review* (1956).
GILBOY, E. W. *Wages in Eighteenth Century England* (1934).

IX *Capital and Finance*

CAIRNCROSS, A. K. 'Capital Formation in the Take-off', *The Economics of Take-off into Sustained Growth* (1963).
CROUZET, F. 'La Formation du Capital en Grande-Bretagne pendant la révolution industrielle', *Second International Conference of Economic History* (1965).
DICKSON, P. G. M. *The Financial Revolution. A Study in the Development of Public Credit, 1688–1756* (1967).
POLLARD, S. 'Fixed Capital in the Industrial Revolution', *Journal of Economic History* (1964).

X *Statistics*

MITCHELL, B. R. and DEANE, P. *Abstract of British Historical Statistics* (1962).